Will You Have Enough?

Estimate and build retirement income

Law Steeple, MBA

Author of *Tax-FREE Retirement*

IAN Books

IAN Books
at Amazon.com, BN.com, Tower.com

Wealth Without Wall Street:
Buy Direct -- Avoid the Commissions, Fees, Loads

The Insiders' Guides to Buying Discount Financial Services:
Buy Direct and Save $3,000 Every Year

Drop Your Insurance:
Buy Only What You Need

*Create Financial Freedom Using Your **Wealth Reserve**™*:
Fix your financial life

The Simple Financial Life:
How to get what you want without going into debt and living
paycheck to paycheck

Build Wealth Without Extra Money or Time:
You don't need to budget or get an extra job

Leah's Money Book:
"I want to control my own money."

The Working Millionaire:
$2,000,000 Tax-FREE **Wealth Reserve**™ Self-insure Self-fund

The New American Retirement System:
a $2,000,000 Tax-FREE Wealth Reserve™
Your Retirement Spending Plan

Long-term Care Insurance:
Is it right for you?

Do Not Buy That Annuity:
Create a Guaranteed Income plus Build your Wealth Reserve™

An IAN Books paperback

Published by
IAN Books
41 Watchung Plaza, B242
Montclair, NJ 07042

Cover photo: Yachts in Watch Hill Cove, RI. by Juliancolton

Special sales for educational use by nonprofits.
IANBooksEditor@Yahoo.com

ISBN-13: 978-1477594087
ISBN-10: 1477594086
Library of Congress Control Number: 2012941177

Contents

Introduction   5

1. Estimate how much income you will have   9

2. How your Tax-FREE **Wealth Reserve**™ works   21

3. Finding the $250 a month to create wealth!   33

4. Self-insure with your **Wealth Reserve**™   37

5. Your **Wealth Reserve**™ as a self-funded 'bank'   45

6. A **Wealth Reserve**™ for Women   51

Conclusion: 65

The Author   67

Introduction

✓ Estimate your retirement income. Make a spending plan.

✓ Create an investment plan for 30 years.

✓ Create a tax-FREE income of $6,000 a month.

✓ Self-insure and self-fund your financial needs.

✓ Avoid tax on 85% of Social Security benefits.

✓ Avoid higher Medicare premiums.

Do you know how much income you will receive in retirement?
Do you know how much you will need to live on in retirement?
Do you know how to invest during retirement?
How much out-of-pocket medical expenses will you have?
How much supplemental income will you need to overcome
  inflation during retirement?

Now is the time to make an estimate of what you will have to spend so you can take action if you need to. Both of you will need to make an estimate separately since one of you is bound to outlast the other.

The good news is that you can assure yourselves of a tax-FREE income since you have started reading this book. I want to help you estimate what your income will be in the future. If you have 15, 20, or 25 years until you stop working, you could accumulate $250,000, $500,00 or $1 million—all tax FREE.

The miracle of compounding

Monthly	Accumulation at 12% per year									
	5	10	15	20	25	30	35	40	45	50
$100	$8,167	$23,004	$49,958	$98,925	$187,884	$349,496	$643,095	$1,176,477	$2,145,469	$3,905,834
$200	$16,334	$46,008	$99,916	$197,850	$375,768	$698,992	$1,286,190	$2,352,954	$4,290,938	$7,811,668
$300	$24,501	$69,012	$149,874	$296,775	$563,652	$1,048,488	$1,929,285	$3,529,431	$6,436,408	$11,717,502
$500	$40,835	$115,020	$249,790	$494,625	$939,420	$1,747,480	$3,215,475	$5,882,385	$10,727,346	$19,529,169

That is possible using the information I will share with you. You know that Social Security will eventually run out of money. You know that income taxes will increase to pay for years of tax cuts and two wars.

Today you can make sure you are protected by creating an inflation-proof investment plan. You can enter your retirement knowing how you are going to manage it. Two-thirds of pre-retirees don't have a clue.

We all know that the old-style pensions are disappearing as employers shift to self-directed retirement plans. Also, we have had less money to build our nest eggs. Wages have declined and unless you are self-employed or work a second job, you have found it hard to amass the funds necessary to guaranteed a comfortable income like previous generations.

Worse, if your employer failed, they may have turned your pension plan over to the government at a lower payout than you were expecting. The Pension Benefit Guaranty Corporation pays more than 44 million American workers, but at a reduced rate. If your employer offered no pension plan, you probably had to save and invest on your own. If you did it yourself, I applaud you.

Now you are concerned about having enough in retirement. You need to know how much to spend, how much to invest and which assets to buy. I will guide you through the process as I have others in your situation. You must create two budgets; avoid income taxes as your money grows; and invest in a way that provides tax-FREE income for 30 years or so. You don't need a broker or advisor. In fact, their fees could take 40% of your money over time.

I think we all agree that, the **best guarantee of lifelong security is having money**. If you built a nest egg of $2,000,000 during your working years, you could probably take $100,000 a year without running out of money. You could leave a legacy.

Whatever amount you have at the time of retirement is important. Even millionaires have to rely on a budget and strategic investing to make their money last as long as they do. The investment strategy you use in retirement is more important than the one you used before. It will determine how much you can spend and how long it will last.

> Money provides lifelong security

I assume you made contributions to a retirement account at work or on your own. I assume you will have income from Social Security and perhaps a pension from an employer, a rollover IRA from a former pension plan and some investments. All of these sources of income are taxable. Your first objective is to consider converting some of these into **tax-FREE** income sources in retirement.

In retirement, you want to avoid paying income taxes as long as possible. There is a trust account, my colleague Dan Keppel calls a **Wealth Reserve**™, that can provide tax-FREE growth and income. This is a great strategy, especially in retirement! It uses the most powerful financial force available—**compounding** of high earnings over time. It avoids the greatest **killer** of wealth-building—TAXES. You pay **no taxes** on the accumulations and **no taxes** on the withdrawals later. And you don't pay lawyer or advisor fees either. You pay less tax on other income too.

You let compounding work its miracle over time. You or your spouse may need income for over 30 years. A $6,000 deposit each year can grow to $250,000 in 15 years, $500,000 in 21. You create your own guaranteed retirement supplement/long-term care insurance/legacy all in one fund—a **Wealth Reserve**™. You protect both of your futures. You self-fund and self-insure your lifestyle needs in order to save money you will need later.

First you set up the tax-FREE trust at no cost. It is an IRS-approved tax shelter so you pay no taxes in retirement. You can 'borrow' the contributions to your **Wealth Reserve**™ anytime. Think of it as your own 'bank'. You can pay for large purchases without paying interest. You need to pay your 'bank' back so you can have enough in retirement without being in debt. You can manage your **Wealth Reserve**™ in 1 hour once a year. You will know what you can spend for the rest of your life.

I will show you how to estimate your retirement income and revise your estimate each year. When you know where you will be during retirement, you can make sound financial decisions. Financial freedom will be yours.

Once you have an idea of how much income you will have, you can see how much you may need to do what you want in retirement. You may set new goals which will guide your spending and investing habits now. To have enough assets to support your lifestyle for 30 years or more requires that you invest consistently for the long-term. It takes only an hour to set up my plan. It takes only 1 hour per year to manage your **Wealth Reserve**™. You don't pick stocks or bonds. You don't chase yield. You don't buy and sell. You invest for the long term since you have over 30 years.

If you decide that you will need more income in retirement, it is good to start creating tax-FREE funds immediately. It takes time to to cultivate the assets you need—assets that "grow by themselves." You can buy high-earning assets that grow tax-FREE and later provide tax-FREE income for as long as you live.

My clients learned that they can invest the money they were wasting on products they didn't need. They learned the role of risk and reward in everyday decision-making. For instance, why pay hundreds of dollars extra for low-deductible car and home insurance when you are already self-insured by your **Wealth Reserve**™? If you carry large deductibles on all policies and accounts, you save thousands that can increase your net worth. You

For each $50 we save, Uncle Sam "gives" us $19 in TAX-FREE gains.

buy only what you need—catastrophic risk insurance. The best protection is having assets that "grow by themselves."

My clients learned how to value the things they bought. Instead of buying a new car, they purchased used luxury. They turned the things they love to do into small businesses so they could save on many expenses. They planned their purchases to save big.

They learned that their security came from owning assets that "grow by themselves." They felt more secure by making a spending plan for each of them so that no matter what happened they would thrive together and individually.

You can get started today. It only takes a phone call. Your future is in your own hands no matter how much income you have to work with now.

No one else can do it for you!

1

Estimate how much income you will have

A 2002 survey of working and retired pension participants provides reassurance for people who **spend time planning** for retirement. Those who actually plan tend to have fewer surprises regarding spending needs in retirement than those who don't plan. Tiaa-crefInstitute.org

Obviously, the more assets you have available, the more you will have to spend. But even millionaires have to plan because you want to **guarantee income** for the rest of your lives. You have an equal chance of living to age 95 as living to age 70 by the time you reach age 65 (7.8% vs. 7.7%). Women are more likely to live longer. "The fact that the actual length of a retirement period could be 5 years or 30 years dramatically impacts the sustainability of a spending plan," according to the authors of a 2007 study. So, plan for 30 years.

> A plan assures you will have enough to spend for ever

You may think that expenses will go down in retirement. Surveys show that actual spending cuts were less than expected— we spend more! Only 30% of retirees actually experienced a drop in spending. We cannot assume expenses will go down because of inflation and the cost of medical care continues to climb. You may want to continue working and add to your **Wealth Reserve**™.

Market performance has a lot to do with spending levels in retirement. The more of your nest egg that is invested in equities, the more likely your retirement spending will be higher than expected. On the other hand, retirees with no market holdings reported retirement spending in line with expectations—less. Bank CD rates match inflation. The survey shows that people who plan are less surprised about spending patterns in retirement.

You know how little our savings grows when we put it in a bank—1% to 2%. Then, every year, we are forced to pay taxes, year after year. This is why many people run out of money in retirement. Putting all your retirement money into "secure" vehicles like bank CDs, savings and money market accounts will **guarantee you will lose** purchasing power over time.

Our estimate of income in the future must contend with inflation. Remember, at 3%, the historical average, your spending power is cut in half in 20-25 years. Luckily, your Social Security benefits increase with inflation. However, most pensions, annuities and other fixed payments do not. We have to make our estimate of future income in terms of what it is worth today.

This kind of math is called the "time value of money." Here is an example of how we use it in our estimates. Let us say you are not working now. How much does it cost you to live? The median household income is about $50,000. We spend most it so let's use that number.

How could you replace that income? Most advisors say you would need $1 million invested in securities to safely assume you would have $50,000 for the rest of your life. However, we know that $1 million is not worth what it used to be worth. Or to look at it another way, with inflation at 3%, you would need $100,000 in 20 years in order to live at the same level—$50,000—as today.

Your advisor would tell you that you need to grow your $1 million to $2 million over time. That would not be hard since your securities can earn 8%. You can take 5% and still be able to outdistance inflation over 20 years.

Recently, the formulas for doing the calculations of how long your **invested** money will last have been made available to anyone. You can play with them just like your advisor does at https://www3.troweprice.com/ric/ricweb/public/ric.do

By simulating 500 hypothetical future economic scenarios, the calculator can help you assess how likely a stock/bond allocation of your securities will last for 30 years. The formulas take into account inflation and the earnings from the securities you own.

In addition, most people want to know how long they will live and scientists have made a formula for that too. You can estimate your life expectancy at http://gosset.wharton.upenn.edu/mortality/perl/CalcForm.html

So if you were working with an advisor, the easy answer to the question of retirement income is "you need $1 million." The advisor would want to take over your current 401k and other investments so they could receive a fee of 1% or more annually.

In real life, most people don't do that. Since you or your spouse will probably need income for 30 years after you stop working full time, you need to carry out the process yourself so it includes your real numbers. You can predict as well as an advisor.

According to the best estimates I can find, the average retirement asset level is $100,000 to $200,000 for middle-age workers. This amount may double by the time we stop working full time in 10 to 20 years. Most workers do not invest aggressively even when they have the time to benefit from long-term investing. We have to assume the level of assets will be $200,000 to $400,000 at the beginning of our 30 year retirement.

Next, we must estimate our Social Security benefits. I must assume the benefits will be at the same level as today even though we can't know for certain. The people who make estimates of the funding of Social Security said in 2010 that the current levels cannot be sustained after 2037.

If you are near age 67 now, your benefits should not change that much. They are easy to estimate since you can easily find the answer. Use the calculator at http://www.ssa.gov/mystatement/ to find out your monthly income at retirement age and at age 70 in current dollars. The maximum benefit depends on the age you retire. For example, for a worker retiring at age 66 in 2012, the max amount is $2,513. This figure is based on earnings at the maximum taxable amount for every year after age 21.

At the other end of the scale is the minimum. There is no minimum. You can read the formula at http://www.socialsecurity.gov/pubs/10070.html but let's use the average benefit of a worker receiving benefits today. The average monthly Social Security benefit for a retired worker was about $1,230 at the beginning of 2012.

This gives us a baseline for the average household income of $50,000 today. If we assume there are two of you, this makes your income $2,460 a month or about $30,000 a year in today's money. Social Security benefits grow with inflation, so if you retire in the next 20 years, your benefits will be the same percentage of your family income as $30,000 is to $50,000 today.

So we assume that 3/5ths of your combined income will come from Social Security for the rest of your lives unless the benefits are reduced. I am making the assumption that each spouse has equal benefits. In the past this was not the case. However, I think the wage gap is closing and this is a valid assumption for the future.

Where will the other 40% of your income come from? Current retirees receive pensions and work and have assets that cover the balance. I have assumed that most paid pensions will be gone in the next decade. That leaves working and investment assets to generate the remaining $20,000 in today's dollars.

We need to pull together all the old pensions you left at other jobs or that were sent to the government to pay out. Go to http://www.pbgc.gov/wr/trusteed/plans.html and see about your former employer plan. If you were the beneficiary of life insurance from a relative, try the treasurer of the state where they lived. If you moved, check money left with utilities or banks that was sent to the state. Check online with the official site—don't pay someone to look for you. Start here: http://www.missingmoney.com/

Once you locate a pension or lump sum, determine when and how much per month you will receive. Don't spend the lump sum. Unless it triggers increased taxes, add any lump sum to your **Wealth Reserve**™. If there are taxes due on your pension or lump sum, it is better to receive it slowly so it does not put your current income into the next tax bracket. See an accountant.

You need to list all of your sources—past pensions, current IRAs, rollover IRAs (401ks, 403b, profit sharing, etc.), insurance benefits and other possible sources. This will help you establish a current shortfall. If you wait until retirement to estimate, you have less time to improve your situation. It is time not the lottery that can create wealth and secure your future security.

The assumption I made was that the average worker will have assets (other than family home) of $200,000 to $400,000 later. Unfortunately, most people do not invest aggressively so the most annual income available from this source would be $10,000 to $20,000 (5%). However, we know that inflation reduces this income by half so for our estimate in today's dollars, we will have the purchasing power of only $5,000 to $10,000! This creates a shortfall of $10,000 to $20,000 from these assets in the future.

To make up for this shortfall, we need to create another $200,000 to $400,000 for the future. How we do that is the subject of the next chapter. We have time to fill this shortfall because we have at least 15 years. After all, we don't need the extra money all at once on day one of our retirement. We need it in 20 years.

Another source of income that most people cite is working. If part-time work is available for either or both of you, this shortfall will not be difficult to make up. A $10 an hour wage at half-time produces about $10,000. Future income shortfall can be made up by working and I assume the wage rate will rise accordingly. This estimate makes many assumptions and you need to fine-tune it to your situation. However, I have to assume this is possible for you.

In 1998 the average retiree had these income sources:

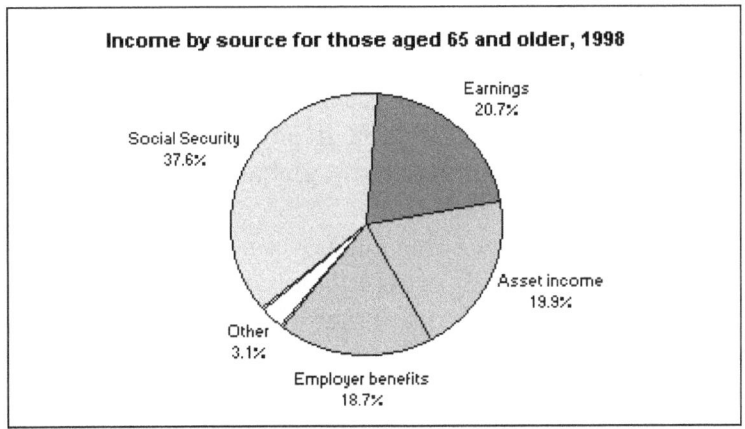

Income by source for those aged 65 and older, 1998

The earnings and pensions accounted for more than in our estimate. If average wages continue to fall relative to inflation, we will not be able to add much to asset income later. This means both spouses would need to work part time or more time.

Another alternative would be to increase assets so more income could be generated from that source. Working could then be optional. On the other hand, most workers today have said they expect to work longer because they lost ground in their 401k or asset building. Some have lost well-paying jobs. Some have used up all their assets during a layoff. However, according to EBRI, 70-80% of workers say they will work part time in retirement but only 27% of current retirees do. We may be forced to work.

If we are going to rely on our assets for income (not working part time), we need to plan to increase our assets WHILE we are still working. This means adding more to our retirement nest egg AND investing in assets that grow at rates higher than bank products. This is contrary to what most people do. They become *more* conservative as they get closer to retirement age.

Second, we can NOT leave our retirement funds in a money market or bond fund, either now or later. They will not generate the 5% or $10,000 to $20,000 we are counting on later. They will not grow faster than inflation. If inflation is 3% and we take 5%, we must earn on average over 8% just to break even during our final 30 years.

Once we leave our employer and transfer our retirement plan assets (401k, 403b, other) to a rollover IRA, we must invest it in such a way that we can receive 5% AND grow the principal over time. The safest way to do this is to invest in a combination of low-cost global equity and bond funds.

I have found a few clients that seem to have found a good mix of funds to do this. They have seen some years when their accounts declined but they have also seen great gains. They have learned that owning the stocks of growing global companies is the only way to stay ahead of inflation.

Many studies have shown that over most 10-year periods, stocks have consistently provided more wealth than any other asset. By investing in mutual funds of different types we can earn more than the 5% we need as income and grow our principal without heavy losses over time.

In fact, **compounding interest and high earnings is key** to maintaining purchasing power over 30 years or more. Investors in stocks, earning 10% on average, do this for the long-term—any period over 10 years. We need to put our money in vehicles that allow our hard-earned money to compound tax-FREE, adding another 15 to 25%. We don't pay tax on it; we spend it.

The **Wealth Reserve**™ does just that. It can compound at about 10% over time and you will not pay tax on the interest and earnings. You can also take out your contributions tax-FREE if needed. If you let your money accumulate, you will have ten times the amount you deposited in about 20 years. If you take your contributions, you don't need to pay tax on them. If you take your earnings after age 59.5, you don't have to pay tax on them either.

Even if you work during retirement, you want your money to grow just by leaving it alone. Its growth is stunted if you spend it or pay tax on it every year. Obviously, this account grows in spurts and can go down in any year. However, over time stock/bond funds can grow exponentially when there is no tax every period.

Alternatively, a bank CD earning 1%-2% cannot provide the 5% income you need nor outpace inflation. A bank account earning 2% while the inflation rate is 3% means that you are actually losing purchasing power over time. Your $200,000 deposit in the bank for 20 years will be worth only $300,000 and provide only $250 a month not the $1,666 you need. Compare that to about $1 million if you use stock/bond funds. Also, since there is no tax due with a **Wealth Reserve**™ when you take the money out, you will be less likely to have to pay tax on your Social Security benefits and other taxable income.

Think of the security you have as you enter your new retirement life. The **Wealth Reserve**™ that you create can be used to guarantee the $10,000 to $20,000 you need and pay for long-term nursing care if you need it or make sure your grandkids go to college or provide a family legacy. When you understand how your **Wealth Reserve**™ works, you can borrow money for current emergencies tax-FREE AND, if you pay back the "loan," you can assure yourself of the money you need for later, whatever comes.

You will have security because your *purchasing power* has grown over time. The problem with a pension and annuity is that the guaranteed income "for life" means you can buy **fewer items per dollar** each month over time.

If you doubt that other people like you invest in the stock market for security, take a look at the long-term returns for various Vanguard mutual funds where they put their money. These funds have provided some of my clients with $1,000,000 or more during their retirement. You could buy all ten Vanguard funds and receive over 11% total return with less risk. When one fund is down, others are up. In 2010, the results were over 15%.

2010 Total Return	Fund	Long-term Return	Longevity
14.9%	500 Index	10.6%*	since 1976
13.4%	Energy	13.3%	since 1984
27.4%	Extended Market	10.6%	since 1987
6.2%	Health	16.6%	since 1984
15.7%	International Growth	11.4%	since 1981
12.9%	PRIMECAP	13.4%	since 1984
27.7%	Small Cap Index	10.5%	since 1960
10.7%	Wellesley Income	10.2%	since 1970
14.8%	Windsor	11.3%	since 1958
10.6%	Windsor II	10.5%	since 1985
15.4%	Average	11.8%	

*Average Annual Returns as of 12/31/10.

However, in 2011, the results were 0% return. The wealthy have learned the ups and downs are NOT final unless they panic and sell. Over time, they are rewarded with total returns of over 10%. TIME works its magic on their **Wealth Reserve**™ funds. Even if you don't have 20 years for your $200,000 retirement fund to grow to $1.7 million, you are better off than having only $300,000. Even if you have only 15 years left before you stop working full time, your **Wealth Reserve**™ fund can accumulate to $1 million.

Even if you start with nothing invested TODAY and you have some TIME, you can build a nice nest egg. If both of you contribute $9 a day, $250 a month, $6,000 a year, to an array of funds like these, you could have $250,000 tax-FREE in 15 years.

In retirement, these funds would continue to grow principal and also produce over a $1,000 a month in tax-FREE income. You can stay invested because you would have your other income sources to pay your basic living expenses. Depending on what you have—SS benefits, pension, IRA—you could leave your **Wealth Reserve**™ funds to grow for a time. The most common reason people run out of money in retirement is that they use too much principal in the early years.

> A
> **WEALTH**
> **RESERVE**
> provides
> tax-FREE
> income

In fact, some clients have turned their 401k into a rollover IRA and then converted pieces of it into a tax-FREE Roth IRA every year, paying income tax as they could. They did not want all their retirement income to be taxable. They did not purchase municipal bonds for tax-exempt interest because they would not be able to increase their purchasing power. Bonds are debt not assets that grow at a higher rate than inflation.

Most retirees have a rollover IRA because they left an employer. You can convert part of that money EACH year, pay the income tax on the amount and deposit it into a converted Roth IRA. If you have no *earned* income, this is the only way to create a tax-FREE **Wealth Reserve**™ for later use.

Alternatively, if you already have a Roth IRA with significant values, you can use it to do your gift and estate planning. You don't have to take the money out beginning at age 70½, unlike the regular IRA. You can let it grow. You can name your grandchild beneficiary which will be effective for both property law and income tax purposes.

Another factor that the inflation rate does not adequately account for is property taxes. In some metro areas, these taxes can take $12,000 a year. Property taxes near Miami went up 46.5% from 2000 to 2004. Will you downsize? Alternatively taxes in Littleton, Colorado went down 1.6% and residents there pay an average of $1850 instead of the $4549 you could pay in Alexandria

VA. You need to decide if living in your current area is affordable given that local taxes are not likely to go down.

On the other hand, while you are making sure that you keep expenses and withdrawals low enough to sustain your retirement, you also need to make sure you are withdrawing enough from retirement accounts to satisfy the IRS. Required minimum withdrawals must be taken from your 401(k) and IRA accounts starting at age 70 1/2. **Wealth Reserve**™ funds (Roth IRAs) are exempt from this requirement. It makes sense to have your custodian or accountant confirm the required minimum distributions or you can calculate them at Imagisoft.com or use the IRS.gov rules, pub. 590, page 33. If you don't need the required amount, pop it into your Roth IRA if you work so you don't ever have to pay tax on the earnings again.

Working longer or working part time can add a cool $100,000 extra to your pot of gold. You are free to quit anytime, especially after a few good years of market returns.

Most of my clients let their **Wealth Reserve**™ continue to grow after they stop working. They can't contribute. However, they know they can't have enough money in the future. Emergencies happen and health cost increase. This fund is your **'lifestyle' insurance**. The miracle of compounding will continue to provide you with financial security from growth.

This review of your plan may indicate that you are in great shape financially. Congratulations. If not, fix it today. It takes **TIME**, not financial advisor wizardry to build wealth. You understand what is needed. We have examples of people who have worked hard to reach a goal that others have considered to be impossible. They play lotto instead of investing just $9 a day, $250 a month. You can start TODAY.

Clients who have enough are those who live below their means, whatever level that may be. Anyone working can become financially independent. We are living longer now. You know you can always use the extra money later on.

Just think of your relatives who are already retired. Do they always have enough? Do they all have a great pension? Do they receive 100% reimbursement on their medical care? Does Medicare cover everything? Are all their prescriptions covered? How about hearing aids? Are medical costs coming down? Have any of your relatives reached 90 years of age? Have any reached age 100? Do any of them have enough?

Most working people know they have to invest more but they think the gap in savings is too great to overcome before retirement. They think that they must save in a "safe" bank account and so they get discouraged. You are not going to make your goals by saving in a bank. Inflation will wipe you out. You don't need to hire an expensive advisor now that you know about low-cost mutual funds that spead you eggs into many baskets.

You can see that the **best gift you can give to yourself** is a Roth IRA invested in a group of stocks over time. Low-cost funds like the 10 Vanguard funds listed at the start of this chapter provide the best chance of maximizing earnings as the market leaders change over time. It won't matter which style or sector is rising or falling at any given time. You would benefit over the long haul. Since stocks have averaged about 10% over time and Vanguard fund costs are low, your account compounds at 10% or more versus 8.5% for funds paying managers with expensive bonuses.

Follow the lead of wealthy successful people—***The Working Millionaires***—Dan Keppel calls them. Invest for your future using the Plan I describe next.

Complete the worksheet below so you know where you stand TODAY and do something about it. You can make your retirement what you want it to be by planning. To build your **Wealth Reserve**™ funds, you need to know how much you need to invest starting TODAY. There is a way!

The Miracle of Compounding

Monthly	Accumulation at 12% per year									
	5	10	15	20	25	30	35	40	45	50
$100	$8,167	$23,004	$49,958	$98,925	$187,884	$349,496	$643,095	$1,176,477	$2,145,469	$3,905,834
$200	$16,334	$46,008	$99,916	$197,850	$375,768	$698,992	$1,286,190	$2,352,954	$4,290,938	$7,811,668
$300	$24,501	$69,012	$149,874	$296,775	$563,652	$1,048,488	$1,929,285	$3,529,431	$6,436,408	$11,717,502
$500	$40,835	$115,020	$249,790	$494,625	$939,420	$1,747,480	$3,215,475	$5,882,385	$10,727,346	$19,529,169

Will you have enough?

Projected monthly income for the average family: Your family:

	(Today's dollar value)	
Social Security (2)	$2,460	$_____
Pensions (2)	$ 525	$_____
IRAs	$ 575	$_____
Securities	$ 440	$_____
Real estate investments	$ 0	$_____
Business or job	$ 0	$_____
Other	$ 0	$_____
Total	$4,000	$_____

Projected monthly expenses for the average family: Your family:

Food	$ 300	$_____
Entertainment	$ 600	$_____
Travel	$ 400	$_____
Utilities	$ 200	$_____
Taxes	$1,000	$_____
Transportation	$ 200	$_____
Insurance	$ 400	$_____
Other	$1,000	$_____
Total	$4,100	$_____

Extra amount needed per month $ 100 $_____

Extra amount needed per year $1,200 $_____

Extra amount needed in 20 years $2,400 (inflation 3%) $_____

Amount invested to produce $2,400 per year: $_____
$250 per month today

Now you each need to do separate budgets as if you were single. Social Security and most pensions are reduced if the payee has passed away. Some expenses will decrease but many like insurance and utilities stay the same. Make copies of this page and complete them. Women have historically had much lower incomes in retirement because they receive lower fixed payments. "Bag lady" fears are not without foundation. Building **Wealth Reserve**™ funds for her is much easier when you have time (compounding) on your side. See chapter 6,. A **Wealth Reserve**™ for Women.

Build your **Wealth Reserve**™ with savings from the Insider's Guides:

o Vehicle Insurance . . save up to $6,000 over 10 years
o Homeowner's Insurance . . . $2,000 over 10 years
o Life Insurance . . . $20,000 over 20 years
o Lawsuit Insurance . . . $3,000 over 10 years
o What NOT to buy: 101 products to avoid
o Health Insurance . . . $5,000 over 10 years
o Disability Insurance . . . $5,000 over 10 years
o Long Term Care . . . $40,000 over 20 years
o Education Funding . . . $20,000 over 18 years
o Retirement Spending . . . $1,000s over 30 years
o Banking . . . $3,000 each year
o Annuities . . . $20,000 in 20 years
o Mutual Funds/Securities . . . $3,000 each year
o Spending Plan: Reach every goal
o Self-Funded 'Bank' . . . $250,000 in 15 years
o Vehicle Purchase . . . $10,000 per vehicle
o Mortgage Purchase . . . $3,000 per contract
o **Wealth Reserve**™ . . . $1,000,000 in 25 years
o Wealth Transfer . . . $20,000 in 10 years
o Living Insurance . . . $120,000 over 20 years
o Self-insurance . . . $20,000 over 20 years
o Business Insurance: Buy only what you need
o Financial Independence for Women
o Survivors: Create Your Future Life

www.TheInsidersGuides.com

2

How your tax-FREE **Wealth Reserve**™ works

Did you find that you might not have enough income for your living standards in the previous chapter? Your best option is to keep working. This has two benefits—it gives you more time to invest for retirement and increases your Social Security benefits. In fact, your benefits increase 132% of the amount at your normal retirement age (67) by waiting until age 70.

Now you can grow additional amounts tax-FREE to supplement your income, pay unforeseen medical expenses, long-term care needs, leave a legacy or make a bequest. You can accumulate $250,000, $500,000 and even $1,000,000 tax FREE by using the **Wealth Reserve**™, a Roth IRA trust account.

It takes only one hour to set up this Plan and only 1 hour per year to manage it. You can contribute up to $5,000, ($6,000 over age 50 2012), but may rise in subsequent years.
http://www.irs.gov/publications/p590/ch02.html

Let's say you will need an extra $100 a month of income when you retire. That is $1,200 a year. We need $2,500 in 20 years due to inflation. That requires a fund of $50,000 at 5%. How will we obtain it if all else stays the same? You can invest $250 a month and have $50,000 in 10 years or $500 a month for $100,000. If you have more time, $60 a month for 20 years will do the trick. Use this chart to get an estimate of what is possible not guaranteed:

Monthly	Accumulation at 12% per year									
	5	10	15	20	25	30	35	40	45	50
$100	$8,167	$23,004	$49,958	$98,925	$187,884	$349,496	$643,095	$1,176,477	$2,145,469	$3,905,834
$200	$16,334	$46,008	$99,916	$197,850	$375,768	$698,992	$1,286,190	$2,352,954	$4,290,938	$7,811,668
$300	$24,501	$69,012	$149,874	$296,775	$563,652	$1,048,488	$1,929,285	$3,529,431	$6,436,408	$11,717,502
$500	$40,835	$115,020	$249,790	$494,625	$939,420	$1,747,480	$3,215,475	$5,882,385	$10,727,346	$19,529,169

If your estimate calls for more eggs in your basket for retirement goals, notice that time has more impact on your final figure than money. For instance, in 20 years, you could have $500,000 or $13,000 extra (in today's dollars) to live on if each of you invested $250 a month. This is possible but not guaranteed. Bank CDs are guaranteed to bring you $3,750 extra a year. Check it yourself:
http://www.moneychimp.com/calculator/compound_interest_calculator.htm

It is possible only if you are using a tax-FREE **Wealth Reserve**™ with a low-cost stock mutual fund inside. You need stocks of global companies in a mutual fund.

Tax-FREE v Taxable

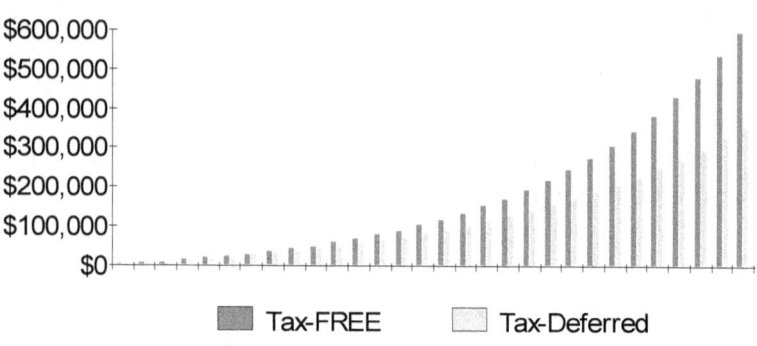

It is possible if you use low-cost mutual funds. This is not my conclusion alone. History's greatest investor, Warren Buffett, told Reuters: "A very low-cost index is going to beat a majority of the amateur-managed money or professionally-managed money."

Many studies have shown that low-cost index funds beat 88% of funds with a stock picking manager. *BusinessWeek* 11/2003. According to a Morningstar study:

"In every single time period and data point tested, low-cost funds beat high-cost funds."

personal.vanguard.com/pdf/morningstar.pdf

Unfortunately, many people don't follow Buffett's advice. They use a "professional" advisor who would never recommend using low-cost index (no commission) funds. Advisors get paid by convincing the public that only "professionals" can pick winning stocks and funds. Most people have not learned the fundamental principle of investing: the **miracle of compounding.** They saved/invested in their bank at 1% or 2% interest rate and "safe" money market funds. They were taught that the stock market is risky and they can't "risk" their retirement money. Some took a chance with a broker and "lost" on the picks—gambling. Some lost money because the fees took most of the earnings.

This is the myth that Wall Street uses to keep most people away from accumulating $1,000,000 **on their own**. No for-profit industry member would advertise that you can beat their mutual fund manager simply by investing in the overall stock market—in a stock market index. No manager is going to tell shareholders that the best predictor of performance is the price they charge. They are certainly NOT going to make a profit if they go around telling people that they are pulling off the greatest rip off in business.

Cost Matters: 0.19% v 1.68%

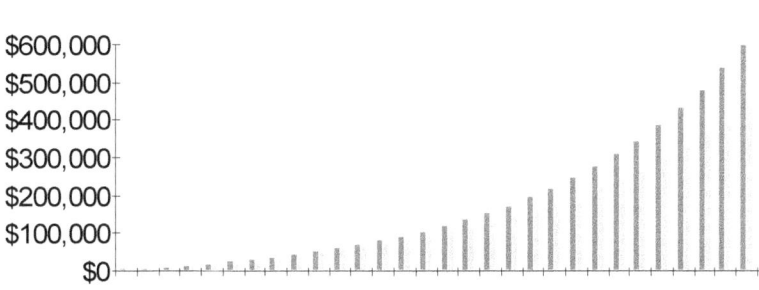

And yet, Bill Gross, another great investor of our time, said just that. During my time in the business, I have learned that like every industry, there are "tricks of the trade" that insiders learn only by being in the business. These include using only the low-cost (no commission/fee) providers. The industry spends a lot of money to influence society to maintain their myths of Wall Street. Otherwise our high schools would teach basic investing principles like low-cost index funds, compounding, dollar cost averaging.

> "Professional money management is a gigantic rip-off."
> Bill Gross, star bond manager,
> *Everything You've Heard About Investing is Wrong*

Most people never learn how compounding of earnings works. In short, we never learn that every $100 is worth $10,000 to us in time if we invest in companies that share their profits with us. A low-cost stock fund helps us earn over 10% per year without losing all our money if one company fails.

Most of us cannot become financially independent without investing in profitable companies. Compare our actual returns from bank CDs to stocks. Our $250 monthly contribution to a CD earns about $180,000 in 40 years. Our **Wealth Reserve**™ would have about $2 million from stocks. I would rather have the $2 million plus or minus $100,000 than $180,000. Which would you want?

This plan requires that we start a **Wealth Reserve**™ Roth IRA trust for free with a low-cost mutual fund company. It requires that we keep making contributions up to $5,000 each year, $6,000 for those over age 50.

A **Wealth Reserve**™ consists of low-cost mutual funds inside a Roth IRA trust account for each of you. The account grows without taxation on the earnings. You may also invest through a retirement plan Roth 401k at work. Since few companies are offering a paid pension, most people are making the investment decisions on their own now anyway.

A **Wealth Reserve**™ refers to the fact that it can also be a Reserve to insure some of our risks. You don't need to waste money on some insurance policies. The Reserve can serve two purposes—a Reserve for unforeseen contingencies and a fund that makes loans and later, provides income to supplement Social Security benefits or Medicare or long-term care.

Long-term care insurance is an example of a waste of money. You will spend $2,500 a year, each, $5,000 together, over 30 years —some $150,000. Very few get to use the coverage. The same contributions to your **Wealth Reserve**™ can yield over $1 million; enough to cover all your extra medical expenses and a legacy.

Unfortunately, we were not taught in school that if we invest **just** 10 percent of our incomes, we could accumulate $1 million to accomplish all that we want to do in life. Our **Wealth Reserve**™ assures us of having enough no matter what happens.

I assume that you do not spend every cent that you earn. If you start investing NOW, you will provide the reserve of perhaps $1 million when you need it. Investing is really about TIME. Consider what would have happened if your parents had invested just $100 a month until you were 18. Your **Wealth Reserve**™ might be $1/2 million by now, depending on the assets they bought. You would certainly have more than you have now.

Start today!

The ***amount of time*** you have to accomplish your goal determines the type of investment you need. Even though we can't predict the day, month and year of ups and downs, the stock market goes up about 10-12% a year, over most 10-year periods.

Range of annual returns of stocks, 1950 – 2000

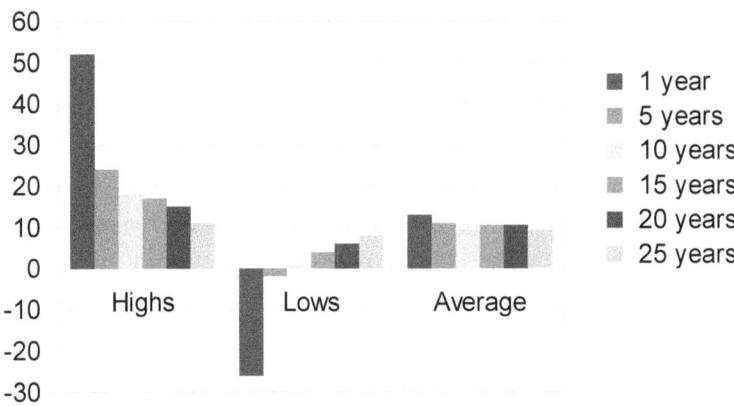

As we saw previously, there are low-cost mutual funds that have earned over 10% for a long time. Of course, there is no guarantee of future returns. Returns in 2011 were 0%, for instance:

2011 Total Return	Fund	Long-term Return*	Longevity
1.97%	500 Index	10.36%	since 1976
-1.74%	Energy	12.71%	since 1984
-3.73%	Extended Market	9.96%	since 1987
11.45%	Health	16.30%	since 1984
-13.68%	International Growth	10.50%	since 1981
-1.84%	PRIMECAP	12.79%	since 1984
-2.80%	Small Cap Index	10.26%	since 1960
9.63%	Wellesley Income	10.16%	since 1970
-4.00%	Windsor	11.00%	since 1958
2.70%	Windsor II	10.18%	since 1985
0.00%	Average	11.42%	

*Average Annual Returns as of 12/31/11.

We must be investors for the long term if we want to have enough in retirement. Retirements last much longer than in the past so we need to keep one step ahead of inflation. This is the reason most pension funds are invested in stocks and bonds. Even though the market fell 22% in 2002 and jumped 29% in 2003, the average was still holding. The chart at the end of this chapter shows market returns from 1950-2010. Your returns are increased even more because you are using a **Wealth Reserve**™ in which your money compounds without current taxes or fees. And it may provide an extra 25% when you take it out since you don't pay federal or (most) state income tax unlike a pension.

This could be considered the perfect investment. Since we have invested in a number of different stock and bond funds, we can have some assurance that we will grow our assets at a rate that beats inflation and provides an income to supplement other income sources. We will earn market returns and not suffer from bad advice from an advisor. Advisors are salespeople not omniscient.

This is the meaning of NOT having all your eggs in one basket. This is a chart of the types of assets. We want to put as much as we can in the top two types—small cap and large cap stocks if we have over 10 years until we need the money. If we are going to need all our money in 1 to 3 years, we are going to put it in the 3rd and 4th types—bonds. The swings are less.

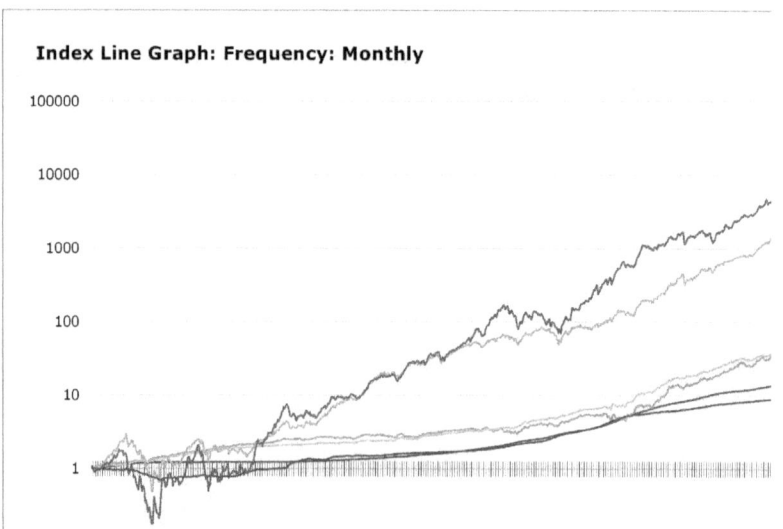

Index Line Graph: Frequency: Monthly

Top line—Small Cap Stocks
2nd line—Large Cap Stocks (S&P 500)
3rd line—US Long-term Corporate Bonds
4th line—Intermediate-term Government Bonds
5th line—US 30 day Government T-bills
6th line—US inflation
Courtesy Dr. Campbell R. Harvey http://www.duke.edu/~charvey/

Turn $9 a day into $1 million

The **key to reaching any money goal is TIME**—not luck or skill —TIME to let the power of compounding work its magic to turn $9 a day into $1 million. Most people will need that $1 million later as our life expectancies grow to 90-100 years.

Monthly	Accumulation at 12% per year									
	5	10	15	20	25	30	35	40	45	50
$100	$8,167	$23,004	$49,958	$98,925	$187,884	$349,496	$643,095	$1,176,477	$2,145,469	$3,905,834
$200	$16,334	$46,008	$99,916	$197,850	$375,768	$698,992	$1,286,190	$2,352,954	$4,290,938	$7,811,668
$300	$24,501	$69,012	$149,874	$296,775	$563,652	$1,048,488	$1,929,285	$3,529,431	$6,436,408	$11,717,502
$500	$40,835	$115,020	$249,790	$494,625	$939,420	$1,747,480	$3,215,475	$5,882,385	$10,727,346	$19,529,169

You can build a $1 million fund in 25 years. You need to invest $500 a month in low-cost stock mutual funds. Since the Roth IRA contribution limit is now $5,000 ($6,000 over age 50), you can build your own $1 million retirement. You may live to age 90.

Start NOW. There will never be a better time.
You can start slowly with $100 a month. You can buy one or all 10 of the funds our clients use. The funds represent the top 4 types of assets. You are investing for the long term even if you only have 10 years before you stop working full time. Why? Because one of you is probably going to make it to age 90.

You might redirect your contributions from an employer non-Roth plan if the employer is not matching it. We have found that tax-FREE income is more valuable later. If you contribute the maximum to your **Wealth Reserve**™ in your final working years, you might make your goal because after you stop contributing, your wealth increases by itself.

For instance, one client put in $6000 each for 15 years and had $1/2 million at the beginning. Then, because they had pensions and rollover IRAs for income, they left most of their future income grow. In six years, when they needed it, they had over $1 million. Why don't you project your own future nest egg with this calculator: moneychimp.com/calculator/compound_interest_calculator.htm

TIME solved their need for income later. They let their money in stocks and bonds grow. Warren Buffett has reminded all of us: "We continue to make more money when *snoring* than when active." Berkshirehathaway.com/

You can implement your strategy by calling one of the low-cost mutual funds like Vanguard, Fidelity or TIAA-CREF. You open a Roth IRA account. You can do it online too. These firms provide the best value for your money since their fees are low.

You can have the licensed telephone person complete the application with you so you get all your questions answered then. Congratulations, you just saved yourself 5.75% of your first year contributions—there are no commissions (loads) with Vanguard.com and TIAA-CREF.org. They are run for your benefit; not owners/managers. Their fees are at cost.

A ROTH IRA allows you to grow the assets without tax ... ever —it's FREE of federal and state income tax as long as you keep it open for five years and withdraw earnings after age 59½. You may even receive a tax CREDIT for $1,000 for your investments.

You will receive a prospectus (owner's manual) for each fund you use. Our clients use the TIAA-CREF Equity Index or the Fidelity Spartan or Vanguard 500 Index to start. These funds have the stocks of very large American companies. Some clients add International Stock or International Equity since they represent markets around the world. The Energy and Health funds already have global giants. Some buy all ten Vanguard funds.

Keep it simple by buying all the funds from one of these mutual fund complexes. You will receive only one statement with your funds' returns listed.

Begin an automatic monthly debit from your checking account on the application. You will pay the lowest share cost over time this way. Most people list their spouse as primary and children as contingent beneficiaries. The telephone representatives is licensed and can answer any questions you have.

This strategy provides you with the **best chance of accumulating** the greatest amount with the least risk over time while not wasting a dime of your money on a high-paid manager. You may use a Roth 401k at work. That Roth 401k works the same way but you can contribute much more to it—in 2012, $17,000. irs.gov/retirement/article/0,,id=232327,00.html

My plan offers asset diversification and "dollar cost averaging," the lowest-cost method of buying the companies you may use everyday—Apple, GE, GM. An advisor is not necessary since you are not interested in chasing last year's hot mutual fund. The expenses are as low as $5 per $10,000 vs. $271 every year for some stock fund manager's high salary and staff. Morningstar.com

Your advisor is not going to agree with this strategy. Wall Street salespeople claim that they can beat the market averages.

And some do for short periods. However, Wall Street insiders know that the averages are hard to beat over time. Most of their money is in low-cost funds or shares of index funds (ETFs). This is especially true in down markets since costs can exceed returns.

Both stock and bond index funds provide better returns than 88% of managed funds for periods greater than 10 years. Low-cost funds don't require you to hope the manager will predict the future correctly. The odds of predicting correctly are 1 in 15,000 each year separately. Over time, all funds provide average returns minus their costs. Investors jump around hot funds and lose over time.

A few managers will beat the average by luck—Just not the same ones every year. nytimes.com/2008/07/13/business/13stra.html You still have to pay the costs of the manager, their staff and operations and advertising whether or not they beat the market. They must beat the market by 1-2%. When they don't you pay. This is why over time, you are going to lose. Costs can take 33% of your returns over time.

Investors with high-paid manager funds LOST **5.73%** in 2011 while the market earned 2.12%. This has happened for 17 years.

As this report has shown for the 17th time in as many years, mutual fund investors consistently underperform the relevant index. The report also shows that most of this loss in performance is due to psychological factors that translate into poor timing of their buys and sells (investor behavior). QAIB 2011

http://www.annuity123.com/Portals/1/whitepapers/F_2011%20QAIB.pdf
http://www.dalbar.com/Portals/dalbar/cache/News/PressReleases/2012%20QAIB%20Press%20Release.pdf

As in any business, mutual fund managers get paid for increasing sales. The manager must compete with thousands of funds. Marketing costs are high. Popular funds grow until they produce average returns with high expenses.

Fund management—structure and governance—are customer-oriented only at Vanguard's and TIAA-CREF. This makes a lot of difference in costs and thus your returns.

Why we use Vanguard and TIAA-CREF

The Vanguard Group, is owned by its 20 million shareholders—NOT by a management company—holding over $1.8 trillion assets for institutions and individuals.

Vanguard offers no-load funds with low operating expenses: $20 for each $10,000 compared with $271 per year for some funds. Over 40 years, your $10,000 index fund may grow to $931,000 versus $453,000 for a managed fund. Vanguard.com **800-252-9578** Apply online: STAR minimum $1,000. Your strategy is to stay invested and not try to time the market—let TIME beat inflation.

TIAA-CREF is the non-profit pension provider for most educational and research institutions. It manages $487 billion in assets with the highest service quality at low cost. Low expenses and low initial contributions make TIAA-CREF a good choice for your investing start. You can make application online and begin immediately with an automatic monthly contribution of $100 or more from their bank account.

Both firms are focused on you, not on manager profits.

You need to write an Investment Policy Statement to guide your investing and control your emotions. This is an important document. It helps you keep your head when the market goes up and when it goes down. Clients lost money when they tried to time the market swings. They could never get it right.

Your Investment Policy is a simple statement: "I will continue my automatic investment option no matter what. I will invest $250 each month in the Vanguard 500 Index or the TIAA-CREF Equity Index. I will not stop investing in that or other equity funds until I reach my goal of $_____. I won't touch the money."

You have a very simple choice. Invest $500 a month in a "safe" bank account and end up with $140,000 in 20 years or $500,000 tax FREE in your **Wealth Reserve**™ Roth IRA trust.

The past provides only PROBABLE futures but isn't $500,000 (plus or minus $100,000) better than $140,000?

Year	Returns	Balance	Balance	Balance	Balance
		$2,000			
1950	31%	$2,620			
1951	24%	$5,729			
1952	18%	$9,120			
1953	-1%	$11,009			
1954	52%	$19,773			
1955	31%	$28,523			
1956	5%	$32,049			
1957	-11%	$30,304			
1958	43%	$46,194			
1959	12%	$53,978			
1960	1%	$56,538			
1961	26%	$73,757			
1962	-8%	$69,697			
1963	24%	$88,904			
1964	16%	$105,449			
1965	12%	$120,342			
1966	-10%	$110,108			
1967	24%	$139,014			
1968	11%	$156,526			
1969	-8%	$145,844	2,000		
1970	4%	$153,757	2,080		
1971	14%	$177,563	4,651		
1972	19%	$213,681	7,915		
1973	-14%	$185,485	8,527		
1974	-26%	$138,739	7,790		
1975	37%	$192,813	13,412		
1976	24%	$241,568	19,111		
1977	-8%	$224,082	19,422		
1978	6%	$239,647	22,707		
1979	18%	$285,144	29,155	2,000	
1980	32%	$379,030	41,124	2,640	
1981	-5%	$361,978	40,968	4,408	
1982	22%	$444,053	52,421	7,818	
1983	21%	$539,724	65,850	11,879	
1984	6%	$574,228	71,921	14,712	
1985	32%	$760,621	97,575	22,060	
1986	19%	$907,519	118,494	28,632	
1987	5%	$954,995	126,519	32,163	
1988	17%	$1,119,684	150,367	39,971	
1989	32%	$1,480,623	201,125	55,402	2,000
1990	-3%	$1,438,144	197,031	55,680	1,940
1991	31%	$1,886,589	260,731	75,560	5,161
1992	8%	$2,039,676	283,749	83,765	7,734
1993	10%	$2,245,843	314,324	94,342	10,708
1994	2%	$2,292,800	322,651	98,268	12,962
1995	38%	$3,166,824	448,018	138,370	20,647
1996	23%	$3,897,654	553,522	172,656	27,856
1997	33%	$5,186,540	738,844	232,292	39,709
1998	28%	$6,641,331	948,281	299,894	53,387
1999	21%	$8,038,430	1,149,839	365,291	67,019
2000	-9%	$7,316,791	1,048,174	334,235	62,807
2001	-12%	$6,447,855	925,203	296,223	57,095
2002	-22%	$5,024,437	722,291	232,316	46,035
2003	29%	$6,459,474	930,787	301,119	61,730
2004	11%	$7,164,483	1,034,274	336,099	70,664
2005	5%	$7,512,677	1,084,540	352,433	74,098
2006	15%	$8,694,884	1,259,259	412,409	90,450
2007	5%	$9,163,538	1,327,133	434,638	95,325
2008	-39%	$5,601,431	813,388	268,074	60,754
2009	27%	$7,116,358	952,155	342,993	79,699
2010	15%	$8,186,112	1,097,278	396,742	93,954
Avg.	12.5%	12.5%	11.48%	13.0%	10.17%

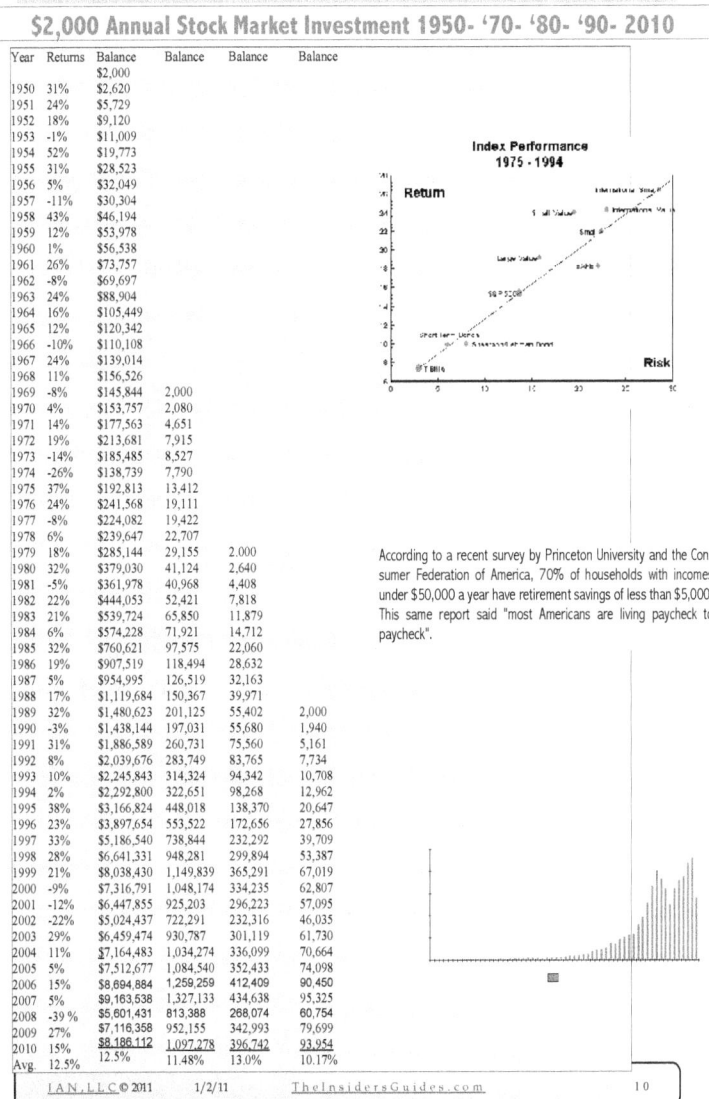

Index Performance 1975 - 1994

According to a recent survey by Princeton University and the Consumer Federation of America, 70% of households with incomes under $50,000 a year have retirement savings of less than $5,000. This same report said "most Americans are living paycheck to paycheck".

Ibbotson Associates **Stocks average 11.4% per year, bonds 5%, CDs 3%.** Stocks have gone up as much as 54% and as low as –43% in 1 year, up to 28% or down to –12% in 5 years, up 20% or down 0% in 10 years, up 18% or up 3% in 20 years. Short term bonds have gone up 14% or up 0% in 1 year, up 11% or up 0% in 5 years, up 9% or up 0% in 10 years, up 10% or up 1% in 20 years. Large cap stocks have had fewer losing years than treasuries or corporate bonds since 1945.

31

The **Wealth Reserve**™ Roth IRA Rules

Contributions:

$5,000 ($6,000 over age 50) each year
Income under $125,000 (2012) single
married $183,000 (2012)

Employer plan Roth 401k
17,000 (2012) each year
No income limit

Distributions:

Tax-FREE for contributions.
And Tax-FREE for earnings if
Over age 591/2,
Account open 5 years,
Taxable earnings unless
Disabled,
First home ($10,000),
Death

Bonus:

Account can grow tax-FREE for life
Minimum distribution rules don't apply
Heirs don't pay income tax
Account has no maximum

Check with your tax preparer
www.IRS.gov/pub/irs-pdf/p590.pdf

3

Finding the $250 a month to create wealth!

You have determined you need to start or add to your **Wealth Reserve**™. You have learned how to invest. Successful investors must learn to be patient in order to cultivate the assets that "grow by themselves." You know you need to buy assets that grow in order to have enough to provide the income for the rest of your lives. Master investor Warren Buffett said:

We continue to make more money when snoring than when active.
Berkshirehathaway.com

Time rewards you if you are patient. Hollywood exploits our childish fantasy of the instant millionaire. Real "working millionaires" don't get rich overnight. The most common method of making money is to use the power of compounding. You need to memorize the following chart so when you panic, you can remind yourself that "this too shall pass."

The miracle of compounding

Monthly	Accumulation at 12% per year									
	5	10	15	20	25	30	35	40	45	50
$100	$8,167	$23,004	$49,958	$98,925	$187,884	$349,496	$643,095	$1,176,477	$2,145,469	$3,905,834
$200	$16,334	$46,008	$99,916	$197,850	$375,768	$698,992	$1,286,190	$2,352,954	$4,290,938	$7,811,668
$300	$24,501	$69,012	$149,874	$296,775	$563,652	$1,048,488	$1,929,285	$3,529,431	$6,436,408	$11,717,502
$500	$40,835	$115,020	$249,790	$494,625	$939,420	$1,747,480	$3,215,475	$5,882,385	$10,727,346	$19,529,169

If you need to accumulate $500,000 in 20 years, you need to find the money to do so. I suggest that both of you establish a tax-favored account, the **Wealth Reserve**™ Roth IRA. You will pay zero taxes when the money is used. That could mean an extra 25% buying power. The only ingredient needed is TIME and $250.

Most people don't have the money or the patience to accumulate large sums of money. The vast majority of people with wealth live below their incomes so they can invest some of what they receive. The wealthy spend less than they earn—that's how they stay wealthy. They can't use the miracle of compounding if they spend their money.

Each $100 invested is worth $10,000 to you in the future

Besides patience, you need to identify the $250 a month so you can reach your goal. There are two ways to find this money. You can earn more or you can redirect what you already spend or could spend.

I will show you what clients have done to find the $250 a month. I assume that if you can earn an extra $6,000 a year from a hobby or second job, you will do that. I assume you will fund each of your **Wealth Reserve**™ accounts.

Let's start with the easy ways to find $3,000. Your tax refund is likely to be over $3,000 since the average is over $3,000. My clients have learned to increase their withholding allowances so that their paychecks are larger each month. They have the trustee deduct the $250 from their checking so they never see the difference in their take home pay. http://www.irs.gov/pub/irs-pdf/fw4.pdf They have their $3,000 refund the year BEFORE.

Pay off credit cards as soon as you can. Forgo all new charges that increase your balance. Work on each credit card (low balance first) until you have saved $100 a month in interest charges. Invest the $100 a month in a new Roth IRA or increase your current one.

If you are overwhelmed by debt, consider Chapter 7 bankruptcy and get a fresh start. One client had over $200,000 in credit card debt and had it canceled. They kept their $500,000 home, cars and retirement accounts of over $500,000. Now, they live on what they earn and have managed to invest $3,000 each for the last few years.

Clients have stopped making new major purchases. They shop around after doing their homework. Depending on the amount needed for a planned purchase, clients are using securities to accumulate the cash they need for major purchases. A balanced mutual fund, like Wellesley, may earn 10% per year with more consistency than a stock-only fund.

> A **WEALTH RESERVE** may have only three funds

I ask clients to keep their financial lives simple by using only one mutual fund family. Some use only three mutual funds for all their needs. Some use 10. Since you are building this account for long-term accumulation, don't speculate.

The Roth IRA account lets you take out earnings if you are disabled without penalty. This means that if you are paying for disability insurance on your own, you can redirect your premiums to your **Wealth Reserve**™ accounts.

Hopefully, a light went off in your brain at this instant. Yes, if you can use your **Wealth Reserve**™ accounts to cover you in case you are disabled, what other insurance types of expenses can you use to make your $250 a month nut?

I am a colleague of Dan Keppel who came up with the idea of using our Insiders Guides to help clients find the money to invest. The fact that many people literally waste $3,000 or more each year on financial products they don't need is our theme.

You can obtain all the Insiders' tips to save in one place now: http://www.theinsidersguides.com/. I will provide a few examples. The most important area of savings is your current mutual fund accounts. Most 401k plans charge more than they need to because the employer is not paying; you are. You couldn't even determine how much you were overpaying until recently. Compare your plan to others: http://www.brightscope.com/401k-rating/367778/Google-Inc/372789/Google-Inc-401K-Savings-Plan/

If you are receiving a match from your employer and you don't want to move your funds to a self-directed rollover IRA, ask your employer plan administrator to consider lower-fee plans. Show them the example of Google's plan for instance. If all else fails, change fund options within the plan to a low-cost stock index fund. Remember, it is TIME that builds wealth so if you can give yourself better returns for the rest of your working years, take it.

One of Dan's clients was able to move their family mutual funds to Vanguard and saved over $3,000 a year in management fees. They were paying about 1.2% of their current account values of $349,000 each year for the last 10 years. That was $4,188 of the current value. Now they pay less than 0.20% or $698 per year. Their retirement fund will be $545,000 greater because they pay 0.2% instead of 1.2% per year until retirement. Compare your present funds to a low-cost leader to see the difference. https://personal.vanguard.com/us/funds/tools

An example of one of my client's accounts with stock funds for the long term is below:

Actual client account, investing $3,000 per year, 1962-2003

24%	3,720
16%	7,795
12%	12,091
-10%	13,582
24%	20,561
11%	26,153
-8%	26,821
4%	31,013
14%	38,775
19%	49,713
-14%	45,333
-26%	35,766
37%	53,110
24%	69,576
-8%	66,770
6%	73,956
18%	90,809
32%	123,827
-5%	120,486
22%	150,653
21%	185,920
6%	200,255
32%	268,297
19%	322,843
5%	342,135
17%	403,808
32%	536,987
-3%	523,787
31%	690,091
8%	748,538
10%	826,692
2%	846,286
38%	1,172,015
23%	1,445,268
33%	1,926,197
28%	2,469,372
21%	2,991,570
-9%	2,725,059
-12%	2,403,420
-22%	1,874,601
29%	2,412,905

4

Self-insure with your **Wealth Reserve**™

There is no better "lifestyle" protection than having money. **Self-insurance doesn't mean buying a lot of insurance**. It means understanding which risks are likely to be devastating to your life and/or assets and buying insurance for ONLY those risks.

Take your car insurance PIP coverage. You don't need it if you have comprehensive medical insurance. PIP benefits won't even be used. You pay for nothing. You don't need many parts of the typical auto policy because you already have many of the benefits. You can save more by raising your deductible, too.

Self-insurance means retaining part of the premiums and risk of any insurance contract. Many businesses self-insure in order to save money and control the risks of running a business. Many businesses self-insure their group life, unemployment compensation and health insurance. The premiums you save earn interest and help you grow your Roth IRA assets. When you need your deductible, you take it from your contributions, tax FREE.

An individual can gain the same advantages by buying high-deductible policies for car, home, health, disability long-term care, and other insurance. Another form of self-insurance is to reduce the amount of term life insurance over time. This is the concept behind **Wealth Reserve**™ accounts. Buy only what you need.

Instead of paying $375 a month for $500,000 permanent life, a term policy costs $15 a month. You build your $1 million **Wealth Reserve**™ accounts with the $360 balance. When the term becomes expensive by age 50, you can cut the coverage in half and use your own assets to self-insure the rest By age 65, your kids are grown and your assets provide an income. NO life insurance is needed.

Your **Wealth Reserve**™ will cover your car and home deductibles as well as your supplemental health and long-term care risks. You can actually **drop some of your insurance**. Your **Wealth Reserve**™ protects you against many losses that are small and infrequent. The purpose of insurance is to transfer the risk of catastrophic loss to an entity that pools smaller premiums from many people to cover one big loss. Many people make the mistake of buying insurance for every single eventuality. Besides complicating your life, this is a waste of money.

Term life insurance insures your life so that your family has an income to survive the transition to a different lifestyle if you are not around. They need a sufficient amount to generate an income to replace yours. For instance, a $500,000 benefit can produce 10 years of $50,000. They may want to pay off all or most of your bills. Anyone under age 50 can buy a 10-year policy for $1 a day. You don't need a separate policy on your mortgage, car loan, credit cards, or home improvement loan as bankers say. You don't need permanent life either, as agents say. You can drop your term when your kids are gone and you both have a $250,000 **Wealth Reserve**™ for retirement.

Your **Wealth Reserve**™ **replaces permanent life insurance** as your security for the future. Almost every adult can purchase insurance *when* they need it. Contrary to industry hype, cash value life insurance is a terrible investment for working people. It may be right for the business owner as a succession fund but it costs too much compared with a Roth IRA shielding low-cost mutual funds.

A **Wealth Reserve**™ serves as your insurance Reserve for the risks that are too small or very unlikely. You buy assets that grow with the premiums you used to waste paying agent commission, insurer overhead, CEO $10 million compensation, etc. You use the Reserve to pay for car and home deductibles since it is only the catastrophic loss of $1,000 or $5,000 that could hurt you. Big losses are rare with modern cars and proper house maintenance.

The Reserve of a **Wealth Reserve**™ pays for your own permanent life insurance, long-term care insurance, and disability insurance coverage. The Wealth of your **Wealth Reserve**™ pays for retirement funding and extra medical expenses you can't foresee because they are so rare. Your **Wealth Reserve**™ allows you to buy liability (car and home) insurance at 30% less. It allows you to not waste your money on risks that are very rare. Long-term care insurance costs up to $120,000 and may never be used.

> A **WEALTH RESERVE** provides lifestyle protection

You need to buy only the products and services you really need. We show you how to do that in the Insider's Guides: banking, mortgage, mutual funds, securities, annuity, life insurance, health insurance, long term care insurance, vehicle insurance, home insurance, lawsuit insurance, vehicle purchases . . . almost any product or service.

You can save up to $3,000 per year using The Insider's Guides. Smart people don't spend that extra $3,000. They buy assets that "grow by themselves." They put their money into their own business or the stocks of public companies. That $3,000 becomes $3,202, then $6,811, then $10,877, until they have about $1,000,000 in 31 years, $2 mil in 37. This is your **Wealth Reserve**™.

I am confident that you will be able to save the $250 a month by buying ONLY the products and services you need. I don't know which ones you need but I know you will save by going through each one you now give away your hard-earned pay to agents, bankers, advisors, brokers, and other middle people.

We advocate that you buy directly from quality providers as our insiders do. (theinsidersguides.com/about_us) By buying only what you need, directly, without the middle-person, you both can identify that $250 a month you need. See the *EasySheet*, below.

How your **Wealth Reserve**™ saves you up to 40%

My clients have used our Insider's Guide to Vehicle Insurance to help them save up to $6,000 over 10 years. We explain that standard vehicle policies charge for coverage that duplicates existing coverage for most people. We explain what you need and don't need and why to keep the deductible high. We show you where to buy if you have a problem in your record, or you have vehicles "at high risk." If you are a safe experienced driver, you can benefit by switching to certain insurers. One of them has been rated No. 1 in customer satisfaction for many years by JD Power and pays YOU dividends. It

John K. of New Jersey spent 20 minutes with his new carrier's call center agent. His premium fell 33% from $2,029.30 to $1,358 for 2 Toyotas with full coverage. The carrier is rated A++ by A.M.Best. Claims service is open 24 hours and it has the same complaint rate as State Farm in New Jersey. A year ago, he saved $567 by switching from another carrier.

has the highest A++ ratings. Why pay extra commission and subsidize other people's poor driving habits?

You may qualify for all 13 categories of savings we list. However, our Insider provides enough "tricks of the trade" to help almost every shopper save hundreds of dollars. For example, a client in Hewlett, NY switched and saved over $1,500 on his three vehicles. Instead of spending that $1,500, he has $125 deducted from his checking account monthly by a low-cost mutual fund trustee. He is using a Roth IRA to shield his earnings from any taxation. His goal is to have an extra $125,000 tax-FREE when he retires to cover his long-term care needs, if any.

His **Wealth Reserve**™ is sufficient to "loan" him the money for the $1,000 deductible on his new vehicle insurance policy, should he need it this year. By next year, the $125 a month savings will cover the possible deductible while he earns the capital gains that his insurer used to keep each year.

A client in Montclair, NJ used our Insider's Guide to Homeowners Insurance to save $5,000 over 10 years. Again, you probably don't need some of the coverage that is hidden in your existing policy. Our Insider explains what you need and don't need, why to keep the deductible high, and when **NOT to call your agent or insurer**. He shows you where to buy if you have a home "at high risk." If you have never had a claim, you may benefit by switching to a "direct writer." Why subsidize others' claims? In some states, you can save 100% or more by using our Insiders' hints.

Another client in Vermont dropped his life insurance after realizing that his adult children did not need the protection any more. Further, after reading Dan's *Your Retirement Spending Plan* he determined to invest aggressively to insure that he would have enough to retire when he wanted to. He used our Guides to save 1% a year on his choice of mutual funds and brokerage firms.

The $156 a month he was spending on life insurance is now buying assets that "grow by themselves." He is increasing his **Wealth Reserve**™ with money he did not need to spend on insurance. Instead of spending the $156 a month, he is investing it to self-insure his lifestyle. He plans to replace his current car in five years. He read our Insider's Guide to Vehicle Purchases and will save about $10,000 on a luxury sedan. Building your **Wealth Reserve**™ protects you against giving money away to banks, especially the $3,000 to $4,000 in interest most people pay every year on credit cards and car loans.

You don't have to have extra money or time

The **Wealth Reserve**™ strategy works because you don't have to *find* NEW money or a second job to build your **Wealth Reserve**™. You use the money you already spend for financial services that you decide you don't need.

WARNING: This book offers a strategy to self-insure and self-fund your financial needs. Our Insider's Guides show you how to drop services you may not need. However, before you change your current accounts, make certain that the alternative plan is in place. Do not close the old account/policy until you have tried the services from your new providers and started your **Wealth Reserve**™.

Our clients are "buy-and-hold" investors. They do not try to time the market by buying the hot stock or fund. That activity only benefits the brokers and leaves the average investor earning much less than a low-cost market index would provide.

Most people use low-cost index funds to keep their **Wealth Reserve**™-building simple. Over a lifetime of investing, it is possible to cover a $1,000 deductible for a car accident. Selling shares in a stock fund inside a Roth IRA account does not create a tax or penalty. Since accidents happen infrequently, you may have saved $200 a year in premium for 10 or more years.

If you are purchasing a house with your accumulations in a **Wealth Reserve**™ you would avoid the mortgage insurance that bankers usually charge those who have less than a 20% down payment. This saved you more money each year.

You can save on your homeowners by picking a $5,000 deductible and not needing expensive extras, like coverage for jewelry or furs. You would save on credit life, disability, unemployment, and PMI insurance that the mortgage bank tried to add on to your mortgage.

To protect your **Wealth Reserve**™ and all your other assets, you need an umbrella liability insurance policy for about $200 a year. It would provide $1,000,000 coverage in case you were sued and needed to pay a lawyer to defend yourself. Even if the accident was your fault, the policy covers the judgment and the lawyer fees too.

You can use the **Wealth Reserve**™ for your emergency fund instead of keeping money in a low-interest account.

Another insurance policy to reconsider is one for disability income. If you are disabled, your **Wealth Reserve**™ can supplement your family income for short periods. Disability for life is very rare and most families have two incomes. Most people just cut back on their entertainment, vacation, and hobbies in order to get by on one salary. If an emergency expense arises, you can always sell shares. There is no tax on the sale unless it involves earnings above your contributions. The penalty is waived.

Some clients have used their **Wealth Reserve**™ to start their own business in retirement. They did not want to work part time for others. The business provided the health insurance they needed to supplement Medicare. It also was another way to add to their **Wealth Reserve**™ since they could deduct many of the normal expenses associated with their activities, including travel.

One put $8,000 a year in a tax-advantaged retirement plan connected with their business instead of buying long-term care insurance. This added $300,000 for any emergency, including remodeling their home for easy access and hiring a home health aide. Worst case, they had assets and a business which helped them with health care expenses. Best case, they had a huge legacy.

Lifestyle Protection

A **Wealth Reserve**™ is **lifestyle protection**. No matter what kind of security you need, having money is the best protection you can have. And now, it is even easier to create a **Wealth Reserve**™ because the Roth IRA allows most working people to use market securities for their important insurance needs without paying any federal and state tax on the earnings—*ever*. Contributions are always tax-FREE. Starting today, you can supplement your pension/IRA money with $1/2 million or so in about 20 years.

We are all living longer and are likely to need the money later. Even late starters can make a **Wealth Reserve**™ of $250,000 to self-insure their lifestyles in retirement. When you use the savings from insurance you don't need, you don't have to budget or find another job. A little planning and shopping for financial products can assure you both of a tax-FREE $25,000 a year for the rest of your lives.

If your **Wealth Reserve**™ is not depleted by extra health care costs in retirement and extra living expenses due to a longer life and higher living costs due to inflation, you have the satisfaction of knowing that your Wealth can pass to heirs on a "stepped-up basis." That means NO INCOME tax to heir, like life insurance. The annuity and regular IRA do not afford heirs this kindness. With an annuity and regular IRA, your heirs will get stuck with the income tax bill on the gains at their tax rate. Your **Wealth Reserve**™ can become a legacy for your families.

Below is the list of savings that Dan's client, the King family, shared with him. They dropped some of the insurance coverage they didn't need—accident, towing and health on their auto insurance, jewels and furs on home insurance, mortgage insurance called PMI, permanent (whole) life. They raised the deductible for their auto and homeowners insurance. They switched mutual fund companies to save annual fees. They are paying off their credit cards and switching to cards with lower fees. They switched banks and cable/telephone contracts. They are adding $600 a month to their **Wealth Reserve**™. They will have enough for emergencies, accident deductibles and home repairs.

Most importantly, the King family will reach their goals: College funds, Vacation home, Small business start up, Travel, Luxury vehicles, Retirement, Foundation creation, and a Legacy.

Finally, we ask all our clients to obtain a legal will to protect their minor children and a power of attorney to protect themselves when they can't speak. These two documents can be executed without a lawyer for under $50. nolo.com/index.cfm. The reason you need a will is simply that it makes it easier to gain custody of your minor child, assets and legacy left by your departed spouse. The reason you need a POA is simply that you need an advocate when you can't make decisions yourself. Usually your spouse will be your advocate. You need a living will for the same reason. The case of Terri Schiavo in 2005 made it clear to all why you don't want Congress deciding what you should have decided yourself.

You must start today. Create your **Wealth Reserve**™ following the steps above. Ruthlessly consider if you really need to pay for each financial product you now pay for. Use The Insiders Guides to decide. They were written by **unbiased advisors** who have nothing to gain from your decisions.

Cast off all the little extras you no longer need. Go through you check book for the last year. It really opens you mind.

EasySheet Where Wealth Reserve™ contributions come from:

Monthly expense savings for the King family:			Your family:
Vehicle insurance (2)	$ 56		$_____
Homeowners insurance	$ 11		$_____
Permanent life insurance	$ 167		$_____
Mutual fund fees	$ 83		$_____
Mortgage insurance PMI	$ 103		$_____
Accident insurance at work	$ 33		$_____
Umbrella liability insurance	$ -18	(bought new)	$_____
Bank fees	$ 10		$_____
Credit card finance charges	$ 125		$_____
Other fees, charges	$ 30		$_____
Total amount saved monthly	**$ 600**		**$_____**
Saved annually	**$7,200**		**$_____**

Possible Wealth Reserve™ for the King family		**Your family:**
Ten year accumulation ($7200 for 10 years at 12%)	$139,403	$_____

Goals
> College funds
> Vacation home

Twenty year accumulation ($7200 for 20 years at 12%)	$599,489	$_____

Goals
> Small business start up
> Travel
> Luxury vehicles

Thirty year accumulation ($7200 for 30 years at 12%)	$2,117,948	$_____

Goals
> Retirement
> Foundation creation
> Legacy

Accumulation estimates assume an investment in a market index fund with the same world economic performance in the future as in the last 50 years. Use this calculator to find how much you can accumulate:
moneychimp.com/calculator/compound_interest_calculator.htm

Your **Wealth Reserve**™ as a self-funded 'bank'
Pay up to 40% less for any item

Instead of buying a car or appliance and paying up to 5 times the price by financing it, pay cash from your **Wealth Reserve**™. The cash from your **Wealth Reserve**™ is special. When your contributions grow by compounding earnings and interest to $250,000 in 15 years, for instance, you can take $20,000 for a used luxury car and know you only spent $7,200 of your hard-earned wages for it. The balance was earnings your assets accumulated by working for you!

This is one reason the wealthy stay wealthy. They pay less because they plan ahead. See our Insider's Guide to Banking to see more examples of NOT paying FIVE times the price for financed items. When you fund your **Wealth Reserve**™, you are creating your self-funded 'bank.' It is the assets you have accumulated that "grow by themselves." The assets allow you to finance your lifestyle purchases instead of giving your hard won income to your credit card banker or lender. Your self-funded 'bank' allows you to provide cash for cars, vacations and your own business start up.

Your self-funded 'bank' helps you become financially independent. The key to growing assets is TIME, not investment skill or fast trading. Financially savvy people buy only the products and services they really need.

They save thousands of dollars per year by using their 'bank' to loan

> ### Saved 40%
> Ms. Lee wanted to buy a duplex for rental income. She needed $60,000 down payment to avoid PMI. She invested $250 per month for 10 years in her 'bank.' She earned $27,456 on her $30,000 deposit. She bought a two family house for $300,000 and her tenant's rent pays for the mortgage and ½ the utilities. Ms. Lee is so thrilled, she saves $500 in her 'bank' so she can buy a bigger property.

themselves the money for insurance deductibles, cars, a home down payment, and any expenses they would normally finance. Smart independents don't waste that money paying interest and fees. Instead, they use their income to buy assets that "grow by themselves." They put their money in their own business, rental real estate and the stocks of public companies.

I have already mentioned the client who moved their mutual funds to Vanguard and saved over $3,000 a year. They will have an extra $1/2 million tax FREE in their retirement fund because of that reduction in fees. Broker-sold 'load' funds are **NOT** better.

How a self-funded 'bank' saves up to 40%

Financially savvy clients have used our Insider's Guide to Vehicle Purchase (in our *Guide to Buying Discount Financial Services*) to help them save $20,000 or more on a luxury vehicle purchase. For example, Dan's client, Danielle bought a three year old Lexus ES 300 for $16,000 cash. She saved 30% by buying a quality used car. She paid cash from her **Wealth Reserve**™.

Note: If she had obtained a 7.5% loan for 5 years, she would have paid $321 per month (Bankrate.com calculator). Total paid: $19,260 for a $16,000 car. She paid cash from her self-funded 'bank.' She used the $321 a month to make money

> ### Save 30% or more
> Danielle of New Jersey spent 40 minutes online to find 3 luxury car candidates within 50 miles of her home. She faxed each seller a bid of $1,000 under the asking price. She got two affirmatives. She found a three-year old Lexus for $16,000. She brought cash within 24 hours of the fax. The dealer's service record was complete.

during those 5 years. Danielle, who set up her 'bank' years ago, earned $26,500 in those 5 years. She did not pay the interest ($3,260) on the loan AND she is ahead by $29,760 less $16,000 or $13,760. This is why the independently wealthy buy luxury *used* cars for cash from their 'bank.' They keep building the 'bank' with contributions invested by the trustee automatically.

Another client in California dropped his life insurance after reading Dan's weekly Alert about people who do NOT need life insurance. He determined to invest aggressively to insure that he would have enough to retire. He used our Insider's Guide to Buying Mutual Funds and Securities to save 1% a year on his choice of mutual funds and brokerage firms. *The Insiders' Guides to Buying Discount Financial Services: Buy Direct and Save $3,000 Every Year* at http://www.theinsidersguides.com/.

The $2,176 he was spending on universal life insurance is now buying assets that "grow by themselves." He is increasing his self-funded 'bank' with money he did not need to spend on insurance. Instead of spending the $2,176, he is investing it. He plans to replace his current car in five years. He read our Insider's Guide to Vehicle Purchases and will save using the tips of our insider—a real car dealer.

Building your self-funded 'bank' protects you against giving money away to banks, especially the $250-$350 in interest most people pay every month on credit cards and car loans. For example, many people will have to pay $161 per month for 10+ years to pay off the average debt of $10,050 at 15%. They will spend at least $19,360 to pay off that $10,050. (If their rate is 25%, they will pay $25,080 for $10,050.) They pay almost **double** for that same $10,050! bankrate.com

But that's not all—THE **REAL COST** IS MORE!

Think of it. If they did not have to use that $161 each month to pay off the $10,050 and $9,310 in interest, they would be able to use the $161 per month to make money. They could have made about *$37,036* in the 10 years using a low-cost stock mutual fund. So the REAL cost of that $10,050 debt is actually $56,396!! The lender gets the $19,360 (to pay the debt over time) and **they gave up** earning $37,036 from the $161 payment per month for 10 years. They gave up the down payment on a house!

That $10,050 in debt costs most people about $56,396!!!
                                        FIVE TIMES MORE

Making $250 per month *work* for 10 years in their self-funded 'bank' can provide about $50,000; enough for a home down payment, car, vacation, etc. You will have contributed $30,000 ($3,000 for 10 years) for that $50,000. You can borrow from your 'bank' to pay cash for anything. It is special cash. Your **'bank' cash is worth 40% more than you paid for it over time.**

You don't have to give up a *latte*

If you pay your self-funded 'bank' back, you can buy more things you need at "40% off." This strategy works because you don't have to **find** new money to build your self-funded 'bank.' You use the money you save from DISCOUNT financial services. Instead of buying a car or appliance on credit and paying up to 5 times the price by financing it, you pay cash. See our Insider's Guide to Banking to avoid paying other bank charges.

WARNING: This Guide offers a strategy to self-fund their financial needs. Our Insider's Guides show you how to drop services you may not need. However, before you change your current accounts, make certain that the alternative plan is in place. Do not close the old account until you have tried the services from your new providers.

A self-funded 'bank' helps you save on all major purchases during your lifetime. You can use it for college funding. Actually, the 529 college savings plans are even better than a **Wealth Reserve**™. You can take all the money out Tax free—even earnings now. Our Insider shows you how to pick the best plan: Insider's Guide to Education Funding. http://www.theinsidersguides.com/

You can use your 'bank' to pay for your first home down payment tax FREE. I already mentioned the 'bank' as your emergency fund. Some clients obtain a home equity line of credit as their emergency backup. It costs them nothing until they use it —no fees or closing costs.

In the same vein, you can use your 'bank' to pay for home repairs, appliances, vehicles, or anything. The only question to consider is whether you can afford to pay it back to your 'bank' even though you don't have to. Some clients have the discipline to do that because they realize they will never have enough for retirement without those extra payments.

You can start your own business with a 'loan' from your 'bank.' As I mentioned, having your own business allows you to deduct many of the normal expenses and create a SEP IRA plan that can take contributions up to $50,000 (2012) each.

You can understand why many clients start their self-funded 'bank' as soon as they hear about it. You can make that dream come true for your life by starting your own 'bank' now.

Some have started a self-funded 'bank' for their grand kids. By putting $2,000 in individual stocks or a stock mutual fund for 8 years before age 25, the child could have almost $40,000 by age

30, \$100,000 by age 40, \$250,000 by age 50, and \$1,000,000 by age 65. This does not interfere with the child's or grandchild's own financial aid or retirement savings plan at work. A Roth IRA makes the money tax FREE.

This self-funded 'bank' provides money for purchasing anything without paying up to 5 times the price in interest and lost earnings. As we have seen, it is easy to create a self-funded 'bank' because the Roth IRA allows most working people to use market securities for their important needs without paying any tax on the earnings—*ever*. The Roth lets you pay for a 1st home and disabilities without any income tax or penalty. Taking your contributions is FREE. If you pay your 'bank' back, you would be able to rebuild that \$1/2 million or so for retirement income tax-FREE.

A self-funded 'bank' can be created even if you did not start early. Late starters can make a self-funded 'bank' of \$250,000 in about 15 years. Late starters can find the \$500 a month contributions just like the King family did—cutting duplicate products and overcharges on their current financial services using our Guides.

If they have repaid their self-funded 'bank' in time, it will provide an income in retirement. You can even provide a self-funded 'bank' to your heirs tax-FREE as a Roth IRA beneficiary.

Start your self-funded 'bank' today. Using this strategy, you can be 'bank' President in 30 minutes. Later, when you have determined that your retirement income is adequate, your self-funded 'bank' can become the basis for your own nonprofit § 501(c)(3) family foundation. http://www.foundationsource.com/

It is the amount we keep that matters!

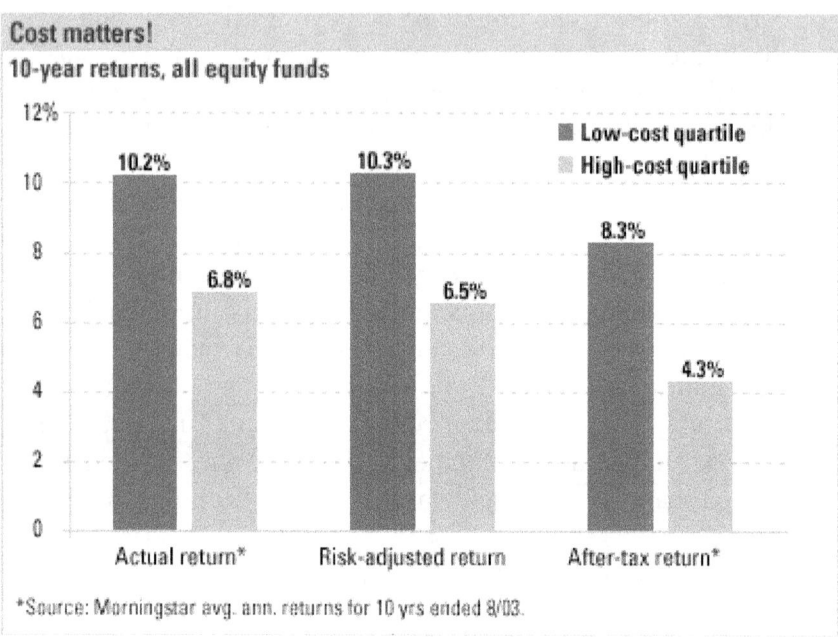

Cost matters!

10-year returns, all equity funds

*Source: Morningstar avg. ann. returns for 10 yrs ended 8/03.

6

A **Wealth Reserve**™ for Women

Women are better investors than men because they are patient. They are the family 'purchasing agent.' However, a woman's average retirement income will be 56 percent less than a man's. They lose over $600,000 in earnings, missed promotions, raises, and benefits. Social Security is the only source of income for 25% of women retirees. Consequently, more retired women than men live below the poverty level.

Women usually don't plan their own retirement income because the family does not realize that they have special retirement needs. They especially need the benefits of their own **Wealth Reserve**™. Without this preparation, many women have ended up in Medicaid long-term care facilities.

Your family needs to make a plan that assures that the woman of the family will have sufficient assets in retirement. Women live longer than men and both of you need to plan an income to age 100. Women need to know about family assets and how income is derived from it so they can manage the assets later.

Women need to make sure they end up with the means to take control of their financial lives. For instance, if they inherit the family wealth, how will they obtain income? How can they tap survivor benefits from previous employers and the government? Will there be enough income to cover the same living expenses? Are all estate and legacy issues clearly spelled out?

The survivor of the family will need to participate in closing the estate and carrying out provisions of the will. Family members need to be guided through the process of asset transfers.

Without their own **Wealth Reserve**™ and the knowledge of how assets are used, women will find this passage bewildering. If your spouse will receive or does receive a pension, you may be the pension beneficiary. Most pensions provide some fraction of the pre-death benefit to you. However, the amount is usually not enough to ensure that you can continue the same lifestyle as before.

Even if there is a life insurance benefit, at death, a lump sum cannot provide for continued income AND a principal large enough to guarantee your long-term health care needs. Establish and fund your own **Wealth Reserve**™ Roth IRA as suggested above. You must be responsible for your own financial future.

Your own **Wealth Reserve**™ creates peace of mind that a large growing asset base can provide income. The key is taking action immediately. It is TIME not investment skill that creates financial independence. You don't need to be genius stock picker. My favorite quote:

"We continue to make more money when snoring than when active."

Warren Buffett, one of the world's best investors berkshirehathaway.com

As I talk to clients who are now on their own, I am more convinced that building your own **Wealth Reserve**™ by simply RE-DIRECTING the cash already spent on financial services does wonders for your confidence. Financially savvy people buy only the financial products and services they really need.

> **WEALTH RESERVE** offers you security in later life

When my clients work together on finding the savings and then buying "assets that grow by themselves," the spouse that had no financial acumen becomes experienced and confident.

It is NOT too late

You may live to age 100 and need income for health or custodial care, so it is not ridiculous to start even at age 60. You have 40 years to accumulate assets and manage them for income. If you receive a pension that you must pay tax on but don't need the money now because of other family income sources, consider letting assets accumulate inside your own **Wealth Reserve**™.

Since you don't know what will happen in the future, this is a prudent act even now. And the assets are not lost as in buying insurance like long-term care insurance. The assets are not turned into taxable inheritance as with a deferred annuity. Your heirs can benefit from the tax-FREE status just as you can. The key is time as I explained above.

> **WEALTH RESERVE** can help even if started late

Women are more likely to lack a personal pension. Women are more likely to lack the experience to manage the family investments. Women are more likely to inherit assets that they do not know how to grow. Although this situation is changing, it has been my experience that many women need to learn how to control their financial lives. Women will have a longer time to make sure their assets will take care of them—producing income far beyond what was originally planned.

Women need to educate themselves NOW about their family assets and why they own them. Families usually own mutual funds, securities and rental real estate in various taxable, tax-deferred and tax-FREE accounts. Some have left employers with retirement plans after years of accumulation. Most of them have opened IRA rollover accounts and had the new trustee move the money so they continue compounding without receiving it and paying tax. Women need to understand how TAX-FREE or deferred compounding works so they can control the supply of income after their spouse passes on. You can't leave this to an advisor.

Many families have mutual fund accounts at five or more different firms. Some members, especially women, have seen their accounts grow dramatically over the years because they don't buy and sell securities as often as men.

Women need to ensure their family has earmarked long-term funding for *their* future financial needs. A family can increase the amount invested by using our Insider's Guides to cut the commissions and fees on their financial service needs.

Financially savvy women have used our Guides to save on all their financial needs. The Guides provide information that sellers don't expect women to have. Thus they are able to gain confidence and power when making purchases of financial products and services. This can be crucial to women later in life because some sellers tend to prey on women who lack financial know how.

WEALTH RESERVE covers your deductibles so you save

Women can be great bargain hunters when they have learned the "tricks of the trade." Remember the story about Danielle buying her Lexus. She knew how to buy what she wanted her way. She found value—quality at the right price.

The **Wealth Reserve**™ Roth IRA is a wealth-building tool that very few people use. Probably because advisors can't charge separately for it and it is really about long-term investing. Advisors are really looking for large sums that they can "manage" for a fee each year. Women have a great advantage when they know how to use the Roth IRA account. Investing without taxation or high fees allows compounding to work its magic over time. This is an advantage that few "professionals" in the industry can overcome.

Once you know how it works, you can amass a huge amount from a small investment. Clients who started late, using a Roth IRA to shield their earnings from any taxation, can have an extra $250,000 tax-FREE to cover long-term care needs later on. If not needed, a survivor can set up her grand kids or her charity.

Earlier I suggested that each of you need to make a plan so that when the time comes, the survivor can know in advance where the income will come from. This is more assuring than a will since it deals with the practical and specific needs of the family.

As retirement progresses, this plan becomes more specific and both of you know how to obtain money—monthly income and emergency money. Some couples actually write down the process in case one becomes indisposed. Even if the survivor seeks help for the executor process or financial management generally, it is good to have a common document as a guide.

Very often, when an estate is settled, the executor's attorney wants to take all the assets into a trust account at a bank of his 'choice.' This creates a lot of fees and problems for the survivor since he or she must then deal with people known only to the attorney. The monthly income deposit to the spending account stops. The trust account must be petitioned for money. All these other people must be paid since they 'manage' the money now. IRAs and pensions that had beneficiary designations don't need to be managed or probated.

You may wish to consult the "Insider's Guide for Survivors" in Dan's **Retirement Spending Plan** so that you can understand the process of executor. With knowledge of how the system works, you may be able to avoid problems that can make your life more difficult. For most people without complicated family structures (multiple marriages, etc), the process does not need an estate attorney and accountant.

How a **Wealth Reserve**™ Roth IRA protects you

I have explained previously how the account works. You can pay for major purchases, insurance deductibles, and some low risk insurance coverage with this plan. You can help your grandchildren start their own **Wealth Reserve**™ Roth IRA with your gifts if you are so situated. They need to have some kind of "income" to qualify for your gifts. You could also split your own account into one for each and make your children/grandchildren the beneficiaries.

You have very deep resources at the larger mutual fund concerns I mentioned above. They act as your trustee for this account and can provide advice and execution, just like a securities firm and lawyer. They have qualified licensed telephone reps to answer all your questions. And they are free.

As I mentioned before, women are three times more likely to need long-term care than men but the risk of staying in a home for many years is small. You are better off self-insuring this risk than buying insurance. More likely, you will need to modify your home or have someone come in to help you with the daily routines. This is what most people prefer and you can plan for this expense.

You may want to consider all the alternatives with our Insider's Guide to Long-term Care Insurance at http://www.theinsidersguides.com/. Your family could waste $4,000 a year for up to 30 years and never use that policy. It would be better to invest those premiums and have the assets for other things if you don't need the expensive care. Besides, 25% of LTC buyers drop it within two years. The premiums keep escalating.

For a woman, a **Wealth Reserve**™ Roth IRA is the security she needs after everyone else in the family has been taken care of. Creating a new life after the loss of your spouse is a whole lot easier when you have a **Wealth Reserve**™.

A **Wealth Reserve**™ for the Survivor

If you are the survivor, this summary of what will happen may help guide you to your new life. Your family may have had different types of accounts. There is usually a life insurance policy, IRA, regular mutual fund accounts, savings' notes (certificates of deposit), bank accounts, and spousal health coverage from a former job. Social Security also provides a small life insurance benefit which you can't collect easily.

You can pay a lawyer to do the assembly of assets or you can do it yourself. Some local Social Security offices insisted that you stand in line in *their* offices to present paperwork. For each type of account, you can contact the institution and ask the procedure for claiming the benefit. Your lawyer would have to do the same thing so it saves money to do it yourself. For many accounts, there is a beneficiary and if you are it, you must follow the rules to avoid creating a taxable event. If you take the money in a lump sum or changing the title of the account to you, you may have a tax bill. Ask the institution's rep or an account.

✓ If your loved one left a deferred annuity, a non-spouse beneficiary may have to pay federal income taxes on the gain. Even small estates may have tax to pay.*
immediateannuities.com/library_articles/taxation_of_nonqual_ann uities.htm
✓ If they left mutual funds, securities, or other assets that have gone up in value, the beneficiary will **NOT** have to pay income taxes on the gains. The estate may have tax to pay.*
✓ Life insurance can provide a legacy at death without income taxes. The estate may have tax to pay.*

*Estate value is assets less debts at death. The portion not taxed by the feds changes annually. IRS.gov Every state has its own rates and processes: bankrate.com/brm/news/news_taxes_home.asp

The life insurance claim form will require a copy of the death certificate. If you don't find premium payments to life insurer but think there was a policy, you can use the MIB's Policy Locator database with 170 million records. You or your attorney can trace life policies to the correct insurance company. Policy Locator provides you with the insurance companies to which the decedent applied for coverage. Cost of a search is $75 at www.policylocator.com.

Insurers don't need to have a copy of the policy to pay the benefit. If you know which company, you may be able to fill in a "lost policy" and claim form online. Usually it is better to take a lump sum and create a separate account for the money at one of the mutual fund firms mentioned above. You will have a consolidated statement and the insurance company will not be taking a haircut on your money. For instance, MetLife says about its "TCA" account that it will use your money to "make a profit."

Your spouse's IRA accounts may require you to compose a letter with the vital statistics of the heirs. Each heir has to take the forms to their local bank for a 'signature guarantee' by a bank officer. Another form required notary signature identification. Another required the death certificate which they kindly returned after making a copy. The mutual fund firms required their form and a death certificate and an account number to transfer the money into. You should make sure there is no tax due on a withdrawal of these funds. You should consult an accountant if you have any doubts. Tell your attorney which account to put it in if you are using the same fund. Otherwise they will put it in a trust company and you will pay fees to the lawyer and the trust firm.

If you are lucky and only have a few liquid assets, you can put the smaller amounts in the estate checking account to pay expenses immediately. Larger amounts could go to the heirs after the estate files a form with the probate court. Depending on how accounts were titled and invested, some assets were held solely by the decedent and so would pass on to heirs at a stepped-up basis without income tax due. nolo.com/definition.cfm.

For instance, if the deceased owned their own car, the will may direct that it be sold. It can be sold to one of the heirs at fair market price and the check paid to the estate account. This would take care of the final expenses and all heirs have equal portions.

The family home may be held jointly and go to you by title. If the home is to be sold, you need to contact at least three real estate brokers in the area. You don't want a low ball broker. You want to interview them in person and understand the important selling points of the house. For instance, the house may be near a small grove of trees or the local grade school. Use the internet to find comparable sale prices.

Finally, after identifying or obtaining the value of all the assets of the estate, you complete and sign the Appraisement of the Estate. This document tells the probate what kinds and amounts of assets are in the estate generally and who the heirs are. It does not require an inventory of the household goods because the value is under a certain amount in some states. **You may never have to probate the will** if you title the assets correctly and have no minor children. For instance, pay on death--POD and survivor accounts, pensions, annuities and IRAs are **not probated** if they have a beneficiary designated. A **will is useful to designate your executor and custodian** of your minor children.

You can transfer many kinds of assets to your family before death. One client bought a single payment life insurance policy for

$50,000. The benefit of about $150,000 would be split equally to her four grandchildren as her legacy. She did this outside of her will and probate. Her kids were the owners. The grandchildren or their guardians will have access to the funds within 30 days.

Another way to transfer assets is to leave securities in a taxable account. At death the value goes to heirs after estate tax if any. You can still use the assets for long-term care, if needed. If not, the heirs will pay no federal income tax on the "stepped up" basis.

You both should not leave a <u>deferred</u> annuity untapped. The beneficiary will have to pay income tax at their rates. You should "annuitized" it before death. Monthly income from the annuity can be used to buy life insurance or mutual funds inside **Wealth Reserve**™ Roth IRA for benefits that are totally tax-FREE.

An IRA left to any person other than the spouse may have <u>tax</u> problems. If you are the surviving spouse, you can use it like your own IRA--pay tax when you withdraw funds.

You can plan how assets are titled to avoid estate tax and beneficiary income tax problems. The complexity and size of the assets begs for an estate attorney and accountant.

If one of you has hereditary indications that your lifespan may be shorter, you can arrange the assets for the most favorable outcome. The assets can be passed to the family without the possibility of the assets being confiscated by creditors, the government or taxed excessively.

You can make sure there will be assets for income after death. You can grow assets for income and emergencies. You can title assets for heirs that avoids estate taxation. You can gift assets to heirs each year without gift tax before the event.

The executor pays all final expenses and distributes all assets by will or account beneficiary. The estate is closed in about 9 months. The final distribution of assets and accounting to the probate take place in different ways depending on local custom. The estate may have a number of tax returns to be done.

You make your own future

When the estate is closed, your new financial life begins. Now you must learn to handle not only your inheritance but perhaps your new financial responsibilities. Take control of your own future. Avoid listening to any sellers of financial products. They target heirs. You need to continue the plan you devised together. All financial firms are pushing annuities today. Guess what? Sellers receive 14% or more (bankrate.com) of the deposit.

If you need the income now—replace a pension that ended—you have two ways to be assured of automatic deposits to your account. You can make a one time purchase of an immediate income annuity from an insurance company. You need to learn more about these annuities using our "Insider's Guide to Buying an Annuity" in Dan's *Your Retirement Spending Plan.* Beware costs! http://www.amazon.com/Your-Retirement-Spending-Plan-enough/dp/1461084016.

You can also just ask the trustee of your **Wealth Reserve**™ Roth IRA to make the payments directly to your spending account. You need to consider how much income you need to replace in order to buy the income annuity. It will deposit the same amount every month. Eventually, that amount will decrease in buying power. You need to have enough assets to grow over time to overcome inflation. Therefore, I suggest you use their old **Wealth Reserve**™ Roth IRA to make up the lost income. Tap into a balanced fund like the Wellesley Income fund.

If you do inherit assets that do not need to be spent down like a pension or IRA at age 70.5, you can put them in a taxable account. This account can be left to heirs without them having income taxes at your passing. If you are working at this time, you can add this money incrementally to your **Wealth Reserve**™. It would be wise not to use these assets as an emergency fund since you need to pay tax on any gains. No taxes are due on your **Wealth Reserve**™ Roth IRA if you are over age 59.5 or are taking contributions.

Using your inheritance to grow your **Wealth Reserve**™ Roth IRA allows you to have the assurance that you will have enough no matter what happens in the future. You also can control the taxes you pay on other incomes that are taxable. If you are not working, the assets grow in a taxable account with little or no current taxation. Owning individual stocks in a taxable account lets you control when you pay capital gains tax. Heirs will pay no tax on the gain.

If your plan included how you will pay for long-term care later, if needed, you can now focus on transferring assets to your children or creating a legacy.

One client with 5 grandchildren wished to provide each with a gift at her death. She was wealthy and the life insurance death benefit would have increased the estate tax bill. She purchased a single payment policy making her 2 sons the owners and their kids the beneficiaries. Her estate will not have to pay tax on the face amount and her grandchildren will share the $1,000,000 tax-free death benefit.

Consider how to transfer your assets to your family with our The Insider's Guide to Wealth Transfer included in Dan's *Your Retirement Spending Plan* book. You can buy tax-managed/efficient funds. $10,000 becomes $25,000 in 10 years at 10%. The funds grow with little current tax and low expenses. Your will designates heirs who pay no income tax on the gain. If you need the funds, the gains are taxed at lower rates. Whole life insurance creates an immediate legacy. At age 60, a $25,000 legacy costs about $33 per month. At age 75, a $20,000 legacy costs about $165 per month. Single payment or modified whole life buys the benefit with one payment. At age 65, a female non-smoker can buy about $66,000 in death benefit for about $20,000 without fluid tests. Don't use annuities.

Trusts are designed to fit specific needs to transfer wealth and control taxation. Living in your home after giving it away or making a reverse mortgage for more income are options. Giving away property now that has increased in value can provide tax deductions and an income for life.

Your time horizon determines your choice of financial instruments. If your life expectancy is more than 10 years, you can maintain control of your assets for emergencies and, at the same time, grow your legacy for your family using tax-managed funds. You pay little income tax now as your tax-managed mutual funds grow. Your family pays NO income tax when the funds are bequeathed to them in your will.

If you want to provide a living gift to your grandchildren now, you can contribute $13,000 per year to their 529 college fund. You can give any number of people $13,000 (2012) or less each year without jeopardizing your estate tax exemption. Use our Insider's Guide to Education Funding to save up to $20,000 in account fees.

You can make annual contributions of up to $5,000 (2012) to a Roth IRA for a young person with earned income. They will have a tax-**FREE** fund of $1 million at age 65. Check chapter 2 of IRS.gov Pub 590 for complete rules for a Roth IRA.

Another strategy is to buy one life insurance policy for all your named beneficiaries outside your will and probate. You can add or subtract names to the list. You can purchase the policy with one payment or periodic payments for the rest of your life.

Deferred annuities offer you, NOT your heirs, the benefits of tax-deferred growth. Unfortunately, your heirs get a big tax bill if you don't begin using these annuities before your will is read. Deferred annuities should be annuitized and the periodic payments used to buy a tax-**FREE** legacy for your family. You can also give them to a charity for a current deduction and income to buy a tax-FREE legacy.

The critical elements

1. Select a company with high financial strength and experience with the product.
2. Make sure the product's strengths and weaknesses fit your plan.
3. Balance inflation risk with market risk. The annual fees rob you of the power of compounding.
4. Know the salesperson, if you don't buy direct. Check the finra.org/ (800.289.9999) and insurance department (NAIC.org).
5. Confirm your understanding of the annual fees and commissions you will pay in writing.

Chart your financial future

✓ Your mutual fund company offers FREE or low-fee planning services.
https://personal.vanguard.com/us/whatweoffer/advice/certifiedfinancialplannerABTest?Link=facet2

✓ You can complete your financial plan using the information above.

Seek a fee-only planner if you don't feel confident you can gain control of your financial life using our information and TheInsidersGuides.com. A financial plan needs to be revised AFTER retirement or income loss in order to make sure you have enough income for the rest of your life. Many people are living to age 100 and need an income for 30 years. Since inflation of 3%

cuts the purchasing power of income by 50% in 25 years, you need to plan how funds are invested to keep pace with your needs.

In a real sense, we all need to keep our investment plan working AFTER retirement begins. Many independent people keep about half of our assets in stock funds through retirement so that they can maintain the same income purchasing power that they had when they began retirement. Many people keep working past age 65 in order to supplement their declining income.

Many financial advisors claim to provide the expertise to manage your portfolio for life. However, there are no guarantees (except the fees). Things happen. Even if you are wealthy, an illness or accident can severely curtail your ability to retain enough assets to live at the same standard for life and leave a legacy too.

A legacy can be created in many ways:

1. Financial assets in a taxable account. Heir pays no income tax. Value is 'stepped-up.' nolo.com/index.cfm
2. Financial assets in a tax-deferred account. Heir pays income tax.
3. Financial assets in a Roth IRA account. Heir pays no income tax.
4. Financial assets in an insurance policy. Heir pays no income tax.
5. Financial assets in a trust. Heir pays no income tax. Trust does.

Stock mutual funds work the hardest for you and your heirs

1. Tax-managed and growth index mutual funds grow with little current taxation.
2. Index funds usually have lower expenses since they buy and hold market securities. Costs vary a lot: 0.05% to 2.71%.
3. The size of your legacy depends on time not just type of asset.
4. Taxes on the accumulation of value are payable only if you sell the funds. Tax on the gains is at a more favorable rate. There are NO INCOME TAXES due when passed to your heirs. Designate "Payable on Death" beneficiary to avoid probate.

5. Funds accumulated inside a Roth IRA for 5 years are tax-FREE after age 59.5.
6. Funds without beneficiary are subject to estate tax and the probate process.

Annuities, IRAs and Pensions

1. There is a maximum contribution, mandatory distribution, income tax payable by your heirs.
2. There are surrender charges, fees, mortality expenses, commissions.
3. There are no medical questions, blood tests, doctor statements, MIB.com reports.
4. Subject to estate tax but not subject to probate process.

Life Insurance

1. There is a maximum contribution, no mandatory distribution, no income tax payable by your heirs.
2. There are surrender charges, annual fees, mortality expenses, commissions.
3. There are medical questions, blood tests, doctor statements, MIB.com reports.
4. Subject to estate tax but not subject to probate process. Check for an unclaimed policy at MIB.com.

Trust assets

1. There is no maximum contribution, no mandatory distribution, and no income tax payable by your heirs.
2. There are initial costs and annual fees.
3. Trust pays income taxes but not subject to probate process.

Long-term investment funds let you keep control of your assets and leave a legacy FREE of income tax to your heirs.

Your Retirement Spending Checklist

1. Keep 12 months of expenses in a low-cost bond or balanced fund (Vanguardcom) linked to your bank account.
https://personal.vanguard.com/us/funds/snapshot?FundId=0502&FundIntExt=INT#hist=tab%3A3

2. Pay down all debt.

3. Keep sufficient auto, home, lawsuit, and health insurance to avoid catastrophic expenses. Use our Insider's Guides on each product to save up to $3,000 annually. For instance, members use a **Wealth Reserve**™ for life, disability and LTC insurance in retirement.

4. Draw down the required amounts of your tax-deferred plans: pensions, 401K, IRA, SEP, and Social Security. There are penalties for not withdrawing the correct amount.

5. Sell assets that have lost ground to offset gains first; then long-term taxable, then tax-deferred account assets, finally tax-free. Sell assets to re-balance your overall stock/bond/cash asset allocation.

6. If you have sufficient income in retirement, arrange to transfer assets to family members so that they do not have to pay your income or estate taxes upon death. Our Insider says that 94% of annuity buyers never use their annuity for income. They pass it to family members who are taxed at higher rates.

7. Establish a small business to do the things you like to do. Your expenses can be deductible from your income and your family gains benefits not available to most retirees. If you need health insurance supplements, educational experiences, travel, transportation, liability insurance, and other lifestyle needs, your business can help provide them.

8. Create and fund your buy/sell business succession plan to avoid dissolution and unequal legacy assets. Ask your accountant.

9. An income annuity will provide a monthly income for life. But you can lose money if interest rates are low when you buy it. It is better to ask your mutual fund family to move a monthly amount into your bank without any annuity fees. You save thousands of dollars in fees and lost interest.

10. Keep investing in stock mutual funds after retirement. You and your heirs pay no income taxes if you use a Roth IRA.

11. Confirm that your assets will not exceed the current federal and state estate tax exemption amount.

Conclusion

Retirement is no different than working when it comes to spending: a budget guides your spending. It is a curious factor in working with wealthy people. The more assets they have the more likely they use a budget to help them decide how to maintain their wealth. Those that don't need it, use it and those that need it, avoid it.

I hope that you have followed my suggestion to make an investment plan and stick with it. A plan will help you avoid losing your nest egg early. The plan helps maintain it for 30 years. When others lose their heads in the market, you have a guideline to follow. It helps remind you of your goals in retirement. There are reasons for doing what you do.

This book is unique in that it helps you take advantage of a unique retirement system—a tax-FREE **Wealth Reserve**™. It provides growth and income without income taxes. If you have time during your earning years to build one or convert your IRA to a Roth IRA, you have solved a big hurdle in retirement spending. You have eliminated taxes on part of your income. When you take the money out for income or expenses, you are not pushing your total income into the next tax bracket. Since I assume taxes will be higher later, this strategy will provide double benefits.

For the next generation, it will be possible to use this tax-FREE **Wealth Reserve**™ as the new American Retirement System. I urge you to give that book, **The New American Retirement System: a $2,000,000 Tax-FREE Wealth Reserve**™ to your young adult kin. It will help them succeed in the new economy. Unless they have wealth already, they will need a guide to create it on their own.

The essence of the system is a self-directed tax-FREE fund you can use to self-insure and self-fund your financial needs. This eliminates taxes on accumulations, interest earned instead of paid, premiums retained instead of given away, and lifestyle security.

Take advantage of the miracle of compounding. Security is achieved by having assets that "grow by themselves." You need income and growth to do what you want to do in retirement. Pursuing your dreams does not end at retirement. Now you have the time. With patience, you will also have the money.

Your Action Plan

This week:
Goal

_____
_____

This month:
Goal

_____
_____

_____
_____

This year:
Goals

_____
_____

_____
_____

_____
_____

_____
_____

_____
_____

_____
_____

The Author

Law Steeple has been in financial services for over 20 years. He was a managing executive of the sales units of a number of bank securities firms. He is the author of ***Tax-FREE Wealth: How to use the tax laws for $2,000,000 free of tax***. He is one of the insiders who contributed to the The Insiders Guides set of buyers' guides edited by Dan Keppel. The guides provide specific ways to save on all financial services. ***The Insiders' Guides to Buying Discount Financial Services: Buy Direct and Save $3,000 Every Year*** is available at Amazon, Barnes and Noble, Abebooks. Law lives in New Jersey and Florida.

To receive Dan Keppel's weekly Alert, go to
www.TheInsidersGuides.com

www.ingramcontent.com/pod-product-compliance
Lightning Source LLC
Chambersburg PA
CBHW071629170526
45166CB00003B/1257